Bad Pennies and Dead Presidents

Bad Pennies and Dead Presidents: Money in Modern American Drama

By

Jon Dietrick

CAMBRIDGE SCHOLARS PUBLISHING

Bad Pennies and Dead Presidents:
Money in Modern American Drama,
by Jon Dietrick

This book first published 2012

Cambridge Scholars Publishing

12 Back Chapman Street, Newcastle upon Tyne, NE6 2XX, UK

British Library Cataloguing in Publication Data
A catalogue record for this book is available from the British Library

ISBN (10): 1-4438-3996-5, ISBN (13): 978-1-4438-3996-9

TABLE OF CONTENTS

Acknowledgments vii

Chapter One 1
Introduction

Chapter Two 15
Blood Money and Bad Pennies: Money and Identity in Sidney Kingsley's *Dead End*

Chapter Three 29
"The Jungle is Dark and Full of Diamonds": Natural Value and Reality Testing in Miller's *Death of a Salesman*

Chapter Four 49
"Real Classical Money": The Dubious Redemption of Economic Life in David Mamet's *American Buffalo*

Chapter Five 69
"New Money" and the Circulating Black Body in August Wilson's *Joe Turner's Come and Gone*

Chapter Six 85
Making it "Real": Verbal, Sexual, and Reproductive Economies in Suzan-Lori Parks's *Topdog/Underdog* and "Red Letter" Plays

Chapter Seven 125
Prospects: Staging Money, and a Note on Authenticity

Notes 131

Bibliography 133

Index 141

ACKNOWLEDGMENTS

I would like to thank my parents Joe and Carol Dietrick for their support both material and moral throughout my working on this project. I also offer heartfelt thanks to my mentor and friend Brenda Murphy of the English Department of the University of Connecticut, whose wisdom, patience, and good humor were—and continue to be—invaluable to me. For insightful comments on earlier drafts of this book I owe a debt of thanks to Bob Tilton, Jerry Phillips, Sam Pickering, and Thom Shea, all of the University of Connecticut. For the gifts of money and time I thank the Babson Faculty Research Fund, of Babson College, and in particular Susan Chern. Since 2008, the BFRF has provided me two summer stipends, a course release, and funds to obtain access to Harvard's Widener Library – all of which have been extremely helpful to me in finishing this book. Most of all I want to thank my wife Kim Freeman, for showing me how to do this and for her love and support.

Parts of this book have appeared in different forms in other publications. Part of chapter three was originally published as "'The Jungle is Dark and Full of Diamonds': Natural Value and the Logic of Naturalism in *Death of a Salesman*" in *Critical Insights: Death of a Salesman,* ed. Brenda Murphy (Ipswich, MA: Salem Press, a division of EBSCO Publishing, 2010. Reprinted by permission of the publisher). Part of chapter four appeared previously in slightly different form as "'Real Classical Money': Naturalism and Mamet's *American Buffalo* in *Twentieth-Century Literature* 52:3 (Fall 2006). The first half of chapter six appeared previously in *American Drama* 16:1 (Winter 2007). The second half of that chapter, on Parks's plays *In the Blood* and *Fucking A,* appeared previously in *Suzan-Lori Parks: Essays on the Plays and Other Works* (© 2010 Edited by Philip C. Kolin by permission of McFarland & Company, Inc., Box 611, Jefferson NC 28640. www.mcfarlandpub.com).

CHAPTER ONE

INTRODUCTION

In his important book, *The Gold Standard and the Logic of Naturalism,* Walter Benn Michaels traces key elements of the worldview of American literary naturalism to an anxiety over issues of material reality and representation – an anxiety that pervaded the gold standard debates of the late nineteenth century. Focusing not on the political differences between the "goldbugs" and silver advocates but on their shared fear of an "insubstantial" paper money, Benn Michaels identifies a cultural logic based on the repression of money as free-floating signifier, which expresses itself in various (and always unsuccessful) strategies of "escape" from the money economy. An aesthetic expression of both the desire for and the impossibility of this escape, naturalism obsesses over the ontological and epistemological questions raised by money, becoming, in Benn Michaels's analysis, "the working out of a set of conflicts between pretty things and curious ones, material and representation, hard money and soft, beast and soul" (173).

The binarism of "hard" and "soft" value Benn Michaels finds inscribed in the gold-standard debates, as well as the fear of an "insubstantial" currency, have of course been explored by other critics. Marc Shell's important work on money in world literature notes that historically, the increasingly arbitrary relationship between money's physical material and its "face value" has made money function as a symbol of a larger disjunction between appearance and reality, seeming and being, "material" and "intellectual currency" (*Money, Language, and Thought* 1). The move, in Shell's phrase, from "the electrum money of ancient Lydia" to "the electronic money of contemporary America," has "precipitated awareness of quandaries about the relationship between face value (intellectual currency) and substantial value (material currency)" (1). Like Benn Michaels, Shell does not only interpret money as symbol within specific texts, but reads money as inescapably implicated in textuality itself, and vice versa. Shell writes that "money, which refers to a system of tropes, is also an 'internal' participant in the logical or semiological organization of language, which itself refers to a system of tropes" (3). Literary texts act as symbolic economies built on "tropic exchanges" (*Economy of Literature* 7).

This same view of text as economy underlies the work of French theorist Jean-Joseph Goux, whose study *Symbolic Economies: After Marx and Freud* traces homologies between the economic notion of money as "general equivalent" – a special commodity that makes all other commodities interchangeable with one another, but itself stands outside this system of exchange – and Freudian (and Lacanian) models of the family and of language. For Goux, the phallus, the father, and language itself function as general equivalents in systems of exchange that are "both economic and significant" (3). The other important homology Goux's work explores is that between what Marx sees as the three historical stages of money – as measure of value, medium of exchange, and means of wealth – and the psychoanalytic categories of the real, the symbolic, and the imaginary. Like Shell and Michaels, Goux cites the gold-money of the nineteenth century as an instance of the fantasy of bringing these three functions together in one object: "At once the *ideal* measure of value, the *symbolic* instrument of exchange, and the *real* means of reserve, gold-money brought together the functions of *archetype,* of *token,* and of *treasure* into a single object." Yet with the advent of "fiat" money (paper, then credit cards, then money that is entirely electronic), the "three functions have come asunder" (114).

The fundamental relation between economic life and both the inner and the social life of the human being underpinning Benn Michaels's, Shell's, and Goux's analyses was given exhaustive treatment in Georg Simmel's 1905 work, *The Philosophy of Money.* In addition to the disjunction between "material" and "face" value later explored by other theorists, Simmel traces two further important characteristics of money. One is money's paradoxical role in what Simmel recognizes as an increasing sense of the relativity of all value. This relativity finds its clearest manifestation in money, which at the same time becomes, in a sense, the only value that is not relative. Money is, first of all, "value turned into substance." As such, money "expresses nothing but the relativity of things that constitute value." At the same time, "money, as the stable pole, contrasts with the eternal movements, fluctuations and equations" of the objects whose value is expressed in money. Simmel puts it this way: "By sublimating the relativity of things, money seems to avoid relativity" (121). Another way of saying this is that money offers a kind of stability, at the price of recognizing the relativity of everything.

A second and related characteristic Simmel associates with money is what he calls the "neutrality" and even "lack of character" of money.

Money is "the value of things without the things themselves." It stands "between individual objects and in equal relation to each of them" (123). More importantly, money lends its characterless-ness to everything it touches – and it touches everything. Simmel illustrates: "The statement that the value of A is I mark has purified A of everything that is not economic, i.e. not an exchange relationship to B, C, D and E [. . .] Everything else that A may be, in itself and independent of this relation, is irrelevant here" (121). Simmel writes that the "absence of any inherent worth in an object cannot be more distinctly expressed than by substituting for it, without any sense of inadequacy, a money equivalent" (123-24).

The practical results of money's phenomenological impact are explored in the final section of *The Philosophy of Money,* which Simmel entitles "The Style of Life." Here, money's relativity and "lack of character" are shown to impart the same qualities to life, with both positive and negative results. One negative result is a modern cynicism Simmel calls "the blasé attitude," a result of "the reduction of the concrete values of life to the mediating value of money"(255). Corollary to this is an increasingly instrumentalist view of the world. Money, for Simmel, is "intrinsically and exclusively instrumental" (Poggi 201). At the same time, money, the absolute *means*, becomes the absolute *end*, thereby reducing all other contents of life to means (i.e. to ways to get money). This in turn gives the modern world "a quality of growing abstractness and artificiality" as an increasing number of things that used to constitute ends in themselves become simply ways to get money (Poggi 209). This instrumentalist view of the world is further encouraged by the increasing dominance of technology that fuels and is fueled by an advanced market economy. As the complexity of technology outpaces the ability of the individual subject to understand that technology (even as that technology plays a larger and larger role in that subject's daily life), individuals must "bracket their own subjectivity and concentrate on tinkering with objects" (Poggi 200).

In Simmel's estimation, then, money is the site of a number of interrelated paradoxes. It is a symbolic manifestation of the cool, "objective" relations between the individual and his world, and it is the means – the only means, the more central it becomes to our lives – to (temporarily) overcome this objectivity through the act of consumption. Money is the symbol of the ultimate valueless-ness of everything, and it is the symbol of value.

There are of course important similarities between Simmel's and Marx's analyses of money, especially in regard to money's alienating and reifying effects. In the "Money" chapter of the *Economic and Philosophic*

Manuscripts of 1844, Marx describes money as "the *pimp* between need and object, between life and man's means of life." As such, money, for Marx, not only conditions the way my needs are turned into actions, but profoundly alters my relation to the world, and to other people. Marx writes, "*that* which mediates *my* life also *mediates* the existence of other men for me. It is for me the *other* person" *(Young Marx* 375). Money's mediating role results in "the inversion and confusion of all human and natural qualities, the bringing together of impossibilities" (377).

Money's most disturbing quality, for Marx, is what one critic calls its "limitless power of becoming" (Sheehan 98). "Through money," writes Marx, "I can have anything the human heart desires. [. . .] What I as a man cannot do, i.e. what all my individual powers cannot do, I can do with the help of *money.*" Yet money's seeming agency is ultimately not one I can control. Money is "the alienated *capacity* of *mankind,*" and as such its great power (and danger) is its tendency to invert the materially real and the abstract:

> *Money,* which is the external, universal *means* and *power* – derived not from man as man and not from human society as society – to turn *imagination into reality* and *reality into mere imagination,* similarly turns *real human and natural power* into abstract representations, and therefore *imperfections* and tormenting phantoms, just as it turns *real imperfections and phantoms* – truly impotent powers which exist only in the individual's fantasy – into *real essential powers* and *abilities.* (*Young Marx* 378)

As this quote illustrates, a primary trope in Marx's rendering of money is that of *monstrosity.* Paul Sheehan explains that for Marx, "Money's capacity for disfigurement, for warping perception and moral efficacy, makes it capable of turning reality into a grotesque distortion of itself" (98). For Marx, this tendency makes money a malevolent force: money leads to "the universal *confusion* and *exchange* of all things, an inverted world, the confusion and exchange of all natural and human qualities" (379). Furthermore, money (in the form of finance capital) is monstrous in its apparent ability to self-generate, to breed itself from itself and to hide its own origins:

> Capital appears as a mysterious and self-creating source of interest — the source of its own increase. [. . .] The result of the entire process of reproduction appears as a property inherent in the thing itself. [. . .] In interest-bearing capital, therefore, this automatic fetish, self-expanding value, money generating money, are brought out in their pure state and in this form it no longer bears the birth-marks of its origin. *(Capital* III, 385)

In describing money as monstrous in this way Marx echoes a theme from

Aristotle's *Politics*. There Aristotle condemns the practice of usury on the grounds that it "makes a gain out of money itself, and not from the natural use of it." The passage continues: "And this term Usury, which means the birth of money from money, is applied to the breeding of money, because the offspring resembles the parent." Unlike Marx and Simmel, both of whose analyses locate monstrous effects in money's interest-generating *and* exchange functions, Aristotle only seems to locate monstrosity in the latter, distinguishing as he does between the "natural" use of money in exchange, and money as interest-generating capital, of which latter Aristotle writes that "of all modes of making money this is the most unnatural" (qtd. in Cannan et al. 105). This Aristotelian distinction forms the crux of the Scholastic conception of interest-bearing capital as an unnatural generation from a "barren" substance, and is essentially the one Antonio invokes in Shakespeare's *The Merchant of Venice,* when he describes Shylock's usury as "a breed for barren metal" (1.3.132).

Aristotle thus distinguishes between a natural and an unnatural economy, between *oikonomia* and *techne chrematisike,* or a "household" economics based on need and its fulfillment, and a chrematistics based on unbounded desire. Of course, such a distinction is difficult to maintain: at the very least we may say that the distinction between need and desire is far from a simple one, that desire is always already a part of what Aristotle may wish to think of as a contained *oikos.* Viewed from the perspective of the work of Benn Michaels, or the work of Marx for that matter, Aristotle's distinction between a natural and an unnatural use of money may seem like an attempt to repress or at least limit money's monstrous characteristics and effects, akin to the nineteenth-century distinction between "natural" gold-money and "unnatural" paper currency. In fact, the association Benn Michaels makes between attempts to "naturalize" money and attempts to limit signification is already recognized in earlier thinking about money that, like Aristotle's writings, marks usury as an "unnatural" use of money. Shell discusses the notion of "verbal usury," and notes that while this idea has been overlooked by modern critics, it is "an important technical term in the Jewish Talmud, in the Christian church fathers, and in the Islamic traditions," where it refers to "the generation of an illegal – the church fathers say unnatural – supplement to verbal meaning by use of such methods as punning and flattering" *(Money, Language, and Thought* 49). As the Aristotlean, Jewish, Christian, and Islamic traditions would attempt to "reign in" monstrous money by naturalizing exchange while placing restrictions or outright prohibitions on the "breeding" of money from money, so would these traditions attempt to limit or repress language's threatening supplementarity.

While I have just grouped together Marx and Benn Michaels in order to contrast their views of money's monstrosity with Aristotle's, there are of course important differences as well between these thinkers' conceptions of money. While Benn Michaels's study may be thought of as broadly Marxist in its demonstrating how money problematizes the relation of appearance to essence, material reality to abstract idea, it is essentially adopting a postmodern stance on that relation. That is, from Benn Michaels's point of view, the problem is not (as it is for Marx) that money monstrously turns the real into the symbolic and the symbolic into the real; rather, money only appears monstrous to the extent that we adhere to an "essentialist" view of that relation. From the perspective of many Marxists, this postmodern view already represents a surrendering to the monstrous distortions of money, and Benn Michaels's notion of the impossibility of "escape" from the money economy would represent the reification of the "economy" and concomitant devaluation of human life.

The decentering effects of money explored by these theorists have had, arguably, an especially profound effect in America, the first country on the planet to institute the widespread use of paper money. In the nineteenth century in America, concerns over the "inessential" character (or the total *lack* of character) of money paralleled concerns over the possible lack of "hard," intrinsic characteristics in nature. The era's obsession with "natural laws" was in fact often applied to the economic realm, where social Darwinism and other views of "human nature" served as justifications for glaring economic inequalities. Writes historian Michael O'Malley, "If physical signs offered one marker of essential identity, possession of money and the virtues it implied offered another" ("Introduction" 370). This use of money as "marker" of essential identity, however, begs an unsettling question:

> But what if the money itself had no fixed character? What if it represented no more than social convenience, or optimism, or paper promises? The answer was the gold (and silver) fetish, the nineteenth-century political economy's insistence on a specie economy and the intrinsic value of precious metal. The essential value of specie, like the essential character of certain races or occupations, helped resolve the ambiguity of identity in public by a resort to "natural facts." (370)

O'Malley's discussion locates this need for a value that *is* what it *represents,* and related anxiety over representative money as a marker of an arbitrary relation between appearance and reality, as a primarily nineteenth-century phenomenon. By the turn of the twentieth century, he writes, "more 'relativistic' or social theories of value and identity" that tended to emphasize "self-making" over natural law gained ground, though such ideas "remain contested today just as they were 150 years ago" (371). The present study is based on the prospect that the conflicts O'Malley traces between natural law and self-making, compulsion and freedom, and representation and reality, conflicts "rooted in the logic of the free market itself"(371), have only deepened in the last hundred years, which have seen an acceleration of the process Simmel, in 1900, already identified as the increasingly rapid "spiritualization" of money (Poggi 161), a telos Goux sees reflected in the once-familiar question, "Cash, Check, or Charge?" ("Cash" 114).

In America, the crash of the stock market in 1929 and its widespread and devastating effects, from unemployment and bank foreclosures to mass homelessness,[1] made the existential implications of an advanced money economy impossible to ignore. The debate between the *laissez-faire* social Darwinists and the New Dealers that dominated the politics of the thirties only underscored the centrality of money in the life of the individual. And perhaps most significantly for this study, Roosevelt's attempt to take the country off the gold standard gave birth to fears of "the end of civilization" (Siracusa and Coleman 29). Through the second half of the twentieth century anxiety over money played out in the ideological battle between the Keynesianism that characterized American economic policy after the Second World War and the "supply-side" and related monetarist philosophies that came to dominate American economics from the 1970's to the present period. Keynes himself had once famously referred to the tying of money to a gold standard as a "barbarous relic" (138). By 1967, however, future Chairman of the Federal Reserve Alan Greenspan, in an essay that appeared first in Ayn Rand's *Objectivist* newsletter and was later reprinted in her volume *Capitalism, the Unknown Ideal,* decried what he called "[a]n almost hysterical antagonism toward the gold standard" (89). A currency tied to gold, argued Greenspan, is our best defense against a "welfare state" that would "confiscate the wealth of the productive members of a society to support a wide variety of welfare schemes" (93). "[G]old and economic freedom," declared Greenspan, "are inseparable" (89).

It was not until 1975, the year in which David Mamet's *American Buffalo* debuted at the Goodman Theatre in Chicago, that President Richard Nixon signed an order allowing gold, for the first time in American history, to be traded freely on the market like any other commodity. By 1978, one year after *American Buffalo* landed on Broadway, economist Jude Wanniski's *The Way the World Works* laid out the tenets of "supply-side" economics, with its fear of an "unstable" currency and call for a return to a version of the gold standard. In 1987,

Greenspan was appointed Fed Chairman, his supply-side ideology dominating American economic policy through the administrations of Reagan, George Herbert Walker Bush, and Bill Clinton, and well into the administration of George W. Bush. Whether or not "supply-side" economics, as is often charged, is a smoke screen for the protection of capital and the disappropriation of the working class, its fear of an excess of "paper" currency not tied to a "tangible asset"[2] shares the nineteenth-century goldbugs' need to believe in a "natural" money – this in an era that has seen even "insubstantial" paper money and plastic credit cards replaced by still less substantial electronic forms. What this logic fears, ironically, is the very nature of money.

The "logic of naturalism" that must recognize all phenomena as either "hard," essential reality or mere representation and nothing else has, Benn Michaels asserts, come to limit the ways we think about aesthetic expression. Just as money, in the essentialist logic of the "hard" money fetishists, must either *be* what it *represents,* or be a worthless piece of paper, the work of art must either be a formal object (words on a page or paint on a canvas) or, in Romantic fashion, somehow must *become* the thing it would represent. Benn Michaels argues that naturalist prose writers like Frank Norris were attracted to writing precisely because it seems to escape this logic: "Neither a formal entity in itself nor an illusionistic image of something else," writing "marks the potential discrepancy between material and identity, the discrepancy that makes money, painting, and, ultimately, persons possible" (Benn Michaels169-70).

If writing, for these reasons, offers an "escape" from the logic of naturalism, drama and theatre offer unique opportunities to problematize this logic. Even more than prose fiction, drama resists being seen as *either* pure signification or "essential" reality. By its very nature drama raises disturbing questions about the relation of signs to the real. Viewed as a work of literature, drama is writing that seems to devalue writing; it is "the form of writing that strives to create the illusion that it is composed of spontaneous speech, a form of writing that paradoxically seems to assert the claim of speech to be a direct conduit to being" (Fuchs 109). As writing that attempts to disguise itself as "natural" speech, drama, much like money, is "ever the presence of the absence and the absence of the presence" (Fuchs 117).

Theatrical performance similarly resists a simple understanding of presence and absence, real and symbolic. Performed at a distinct point in space and time, the theatrical performance is at once the most "real" of the arts and the most radically deceptive – qualities that have often precipitated a deep fear of theatre, or what Jonas Barish has called (in the title of his important work) an "Antitheatrical Prejudice" running through the Western artistic tradition, beginning with Plato. In a section of Barish's study he calls "The Theatre against Itself," the critic looks at the plays of modern authors like Ibsen, Shaw, Chekhov, and Pirandello to show how these playwrights would "build into their very plays a critique of the theater, redeeming their better characters from it as they wished to redeem society at large" (450). Kirk Williams notes that the fear of theatre's "secondariness or supplementarity" informing the antitheatrical prejudice is closely related to anxieties regarding "the binarisms that set essence against appearance, feminine against masculine, writing against speech, fiction against truth" (95). Unsurprisingly given the genre's obsession with these binarisms, Williams calls naturalist drama a "particularly stunning example" of the anti-theatrical prejudice (97). Through its interest in putting "real life" on the stage and its critique of the notion of identity as invented or performed in favor of one shaped by inexorable forces, naturalist drama betrays an anxiety over the very ambiguities that theatrical performance inherently foregrounds and that in turn make theatrical performance possible.

These special qualities of the theatre have made it a uniquely suited medium for exploring related qualities embodied in money. At the same time, the subject of money and the ontological and epistemological questions it raises have offered playwrights a means of expanding how we think about theatre, and ultimately how we think about the nature of representation and its relation to the real. This study begins with a reevaluation of a critically neglected play from the thirties. Largely forgotten today, Sidney Kingsley's 1935 play *Dead End* was seen by many in the 1930's as "*the* depression play" (Casty 234). The play can be read as a less revolutionary critique of capitalism than other plays of its era, and this likely has contributed to the work's resonance with a mostly middle-class theatre- and movie-going audience. But I want to suggest an additional reason for the play's success: *Dead End* is a much more complex meditation on the paradoxes of economic life than either the agit-prop of the earlier Theatre Union or the softened criticism leading up to America's entry into the war. In dramatizing the complicated interrelations between identity and the cash economy in America during a moment of extreme economic and social crisis, *Dead End* identifies money and the increasing commodification of life as both that which traps characters and that which frees them, the fixer and the dissolver of stable identity, going beyond the more explicitly activist drama of the period to explore the existential effects of capitalism.

The naturalistic elements of *Dead End* and the play's thematic attention to money are inextricably bound. With the resurgence of the gold-standard debate in the 1930s (leading up to Roosevelt's effectively ending the gold standard in America in 1933), the issues were remarkably similar to those that characterized the earlier debate. "In both decades," writes Hildegaard Hoeller, "the discussion was not about the actual usefulness of gold reserves" but "about whether gold provided an essential value for money exchange as well as a universal standard of value. Gold stood for a fantasy about a stable referent or reified value; as such, it had become almost an idol or fetish" (766).[3] The Depression loomed large in the imagination of Arthur Miller in a manner that is hard to overstate. A period that saw Miller's father's failure in business and the consequent rapid downward spiral of his immediate family, Miller wrote that the Depression "was only incidentally a matter of money. Rather it was a moral catastrophe, a violent revelation of the hypocrisies behind the façade of American society" (*Timebends* 114). In *Death of a Salesman,* Miller elaborates his own vision of the relation of economic to psychic life by dramatizing the attempted "escape" from the money economy that so obsesses American naturalism – the attempt to "stage the disappearance of money" (Benn Michaels 144). The distinctions that obsess the characters of the play – between saying and doing, seeming and being, technology and nature – are themselves rooted in money.

Throughout the seventies and eighties, no American writer more thoroughly investigated the phenomenology of money than David Mamet, whose work for the stage and the screen relentlessly revisits the theme of economic life and its relation to moral, ontological, and epistemological concerns. In *American Buffalo,* his earliest full-scale investigation of these themes on the stage and what is usually regarded as his first "mature" play, Mamet thematizes the anxieties that will inform all his future work. A careful reading of *American Buffalo* finds what will become the familiar Mamettian conflicts between talk and action, seeming and being, as rooted in the playwright's own complex and often conflicted relationship with a dramatic and literary naturalism informed by the paradoxes of economic life.

The second work in his "Pittsburgh Cycle" chronicling the African American experience throughout the twentieth century, August Wilson's 1984 play *Joe Turner's Come and Gone* is set in the second decade of the century. Wilson's play investigates the interrelated "logics" of money and race, their shared obsession with the relation of immanence to appearance, material value to "face" value.

Suzan-Lori Parks's play *Topdog/Underdog* debuted on Broadway in

2001, during the fourth of Greenspan's unprecedented five terms as Fed Chairman. As a play that investigates, among other subjects, the intersection of "business" and "family" values, *Topdog/Underdog* stands with at least one foot in the naturalist tradition of works by playwrights like Kingsley, Miller, and Mamet. The naturalist obsession with the paradox of human freedom that drives the work of these writers appears again at the heart of Parks's play, and once again money and the confidence game is at the center of that obsession. Throughout the play's often hauntingly repetitive action, money repeatedly emerges as the site of familiar naturalist conflicts between free will and determinism, present and past, the authentic and the mimetic. Through her depiction of two brothers' attempts to variously "escape" the money economy and to become money themselves, Parks elaborates her own vision of the dialectical interdependence of these seeming opposites. In her two "Red Letter" plays, *In the Blood* and *Fucking A,* Parks goes even further to investigate the way money, sexual, and reproductive economies determine each other.

A reading of these five playwrights' work finds not only an increasingly sophisticated treatment of the subject of money, but also an increasingly complex relationship with the tradition of dramatic naturalism. In keeping with a tendency of much American drama of the thirties, Kingsley's *Dead End* is highly naturalistic in its portrayal of the power of economic forces to deform the characters of the play both physically and morally; at the same time, the play's ambivalence regarding the alienating, morally neutralizing effects of money seems to undercut its own naturalistic tendencies. Money monstrously deforms the "self-made," surgically altered, and symbolically orphaned gangster Baby-Face Martin, just as it threatens to deform the group of children who emulate Martin's "ethics." At the same time, Kingsley renders money as vital to the refiguring of the new American family that, at play's end, may point the way out of the "Dead End" of the play's title. Miller's *Death of a Salesman* likewise combines a naturalistic portrayal of economic forces and the moral deformities of "business" values with a complicating of the logic of naturalism. Miller's watershed play answers Kingsley's pragmatic view of economic life with an impassioned critique of American business; yet, that critique is complicated by Miller's almost postmodern treatment of distinctions such as present and past, action and "talk," hard value and soft currency. Mamet's *American Buffalo* is at once more relentlessly naturalistic – in its focus on members of the criminal underclass claustrophobically trapped within their own limited perceptions – and more postmodern in its elaboration of the complex relation of talk to action, seeming to being. *American Buffalo* is perhaps, of all the plays in this study, the angriest at economic life; it is also, oddly, the play that goes furthest to justify money and business. Like the plays by Kingsley, Miller, and Mamet, August Wilson's *Joe Turner's Come and Gone* ultimately must transform the realist mode in order to transcend its positivism concerning these relations. Thus Wilson's play mixes a realist/naturalist style indebted to writers like Dreiser and Norris with what critics have called either a mythic or a magical realist mode. Finally, Parks's plays, again focusing on members of the "lowest" social strata colliding with forces that threaten to proscribe their identities, nevertheless convey a vision of identity, and specifically of racial identity, as *both* "essential" and performed, determined and freely created, complicating a distinction at the heart of literary naturalism.

As does their subject matter, so does the stagecraft of these plays both borrow from and problematize the naturalist tradition. Kingsley's use of subtly metadramatic elements such as role-playing within the role; Miller's (and director Kazan's) use of expressionistic scenery, music, and lighting; Mamet's trademark dialogue at once poetic and realistic; Wilson's emphasis on the performative body and the limits of language; and Parks's use of both metadrama and silence and stage business to convey the "pure true simple state" of the characters: all these techniques work to complicate naturalism's "hard" distinction between signification and the real ("Elements of Style" 17).

Several critics have noted that unlike what has happened in the theatre of other countries, the American theatre has remained dominated by the modes of realism and naturalism throughout the twentieth century, and into the twenty-first. Brenda Murphy, for instance, looks not only at dramatic structure and its persistent realism, but at that same persistent realism in American acting theory (especially the Method), stage design, and costuming (*American Realism and American Drama).* William Demastes, in his book *Beyond Naturalism: A New Realism in American Theatre,* considers the link between this American dramatic realism and the naturalist and positivist philosophies of the nineteenth and early-twentieth centuries. Demastes sees a gradual divergence between American realism and naturalism and some of those movements' philosophical foundations, an evolution toward a "new realism" that could accommodate a philosophy that transcended nineteenth-century positivism to encompass Einsteinian relativity and quantum physics. Demastes points out that instead of abandoning realism and naturalism in the face of a more complicated view of perception, in America, the genres have adapted to make room for this new view. This "new realism" is *self-consciously* naturalistic, and aims to subvert the very model of perception that naturalism has historically reinforced. The new realist playwright uses naturalistic structures toward the end of undermining the positivist view of the world that once gave rise to those very structures.

This study attempts to trace the evolution of the treatment of money and economic life across this route Demastes maps, as the naturalist and realist American play becomes *self-consciously* naturalist and realist with the ultimate aim of undercutting the foundations of these very modes. What we find however is far from a straightforward move from a realism based on nineteenth-century positivism to one encompassing what is essentially a postmodern outlook. Rather, the works discussed here more often express a deep ambivalence regarding money and the logic of naturalism – a desire to transcend that logic and a sense of almost mourning it. The characters demonstrate the performativity of identity, the absence of a stable, "hard" value underneath their money *or* their language. At the same time, they are often haunted by a need to show what's "inside" them, what (in the language of Mamet's salesmen) they are "made of." In this way the characters of these plays resemble the money that they are alternately (sometimes simultaneously) chasing, running from, spending, and hoarding.

CHAPTER TWO

BLOOD MONEY AND BAD PENNIES: MONEY AND IDENTITY IN SIDNEY KINGSLEY'S *DEAD END*

Sidney Kingsley's play *Dead End* appeared during what many critics see as a "middle period" of Depression-era drama, both chronologically and ideologically. R.C. Reynolds divides thirties drama into three phases: "hard-line Marxist drama" of the period 1929-1933, social criticism with a Marxist flavor of the period 1933-1936, and a Popular-Front-era "softening" of the Marxist position in favor of themes of unity and social cooperation on the eve of the second World War (xvi-xxvii). Appearing during Reynolds's second phase, Kingsley's most important work is seen by the critic as "synthesizing the militant ideals of the left with the palatable drama of the commercial theatre" (Reynolds 59). Malcolm Goldstein divides thirties drama into two periods, the second of which, beginning with the 1935-36 season which saw the debut of *Dead End,* is characterized by "a resurgence of optimism caused by New Deal pump-priming measures" as well as a Popular-Front-era softening of the Marxist critique of capitalism that characterized earlier thirties drama (vii-viii). Similarly, Rabkin places the productions of the Group Theatre – of which *Dead End* was one – in the ideological middle ground between the more stridently Marxist Theatre Union and the less revolutionary Federal Theatre Project (29).

Despite, or perhaps because of, Kingsley's being (along with Elmer Rice, Robert E. Sherwood, and Irwin Shaw) a writer of the ideological "middle ground," *Dead End* in its original Broadway production was an unqualified popular success. It followed by two years the playwright's Pulitzer Prize-winning debut, *Men in White*, ran for a very impressive 687 performances on Broadway, received mostly favorable critical reviews at its premiere, and was turned into a successful film.[4] A careful consideration of *Dead End* shows that it offers no easy answers, no clear way forward precisely because its great power is to expose the paradoxes of life in an America where everything and everyone is a commodity. The *Dead End* of the title is not simply the poverty that the play's dual protagonists seem hopeful of escaping by play's end. The term also characterizes, and problematizes, that "escape," the success of which necessitates embracing the very values that lead to the characters' entrapment. At the heart of this paradox is money.

Dead End is, as one reviewer called it, a "Story of Wealth and Poverty Living Together" ("Explosive Play" 17). The setting is a spot on New York's Upper East Side where the squalid poverty of a tenement house abuts the rear entrance of a newly erected luxury condominium complex. It is also, in keeping with the naturalism of the American stage in the thirties, a study of the determinative effects of such inequality. Accordingly, the play focuses on two generations produced by the tenements: a gang of adolescent and pre-adolescent boys, and the adults Pete Gimpty, Baby-Face Martin, and Drina. Each generation possesses a character with a strong sense of decency and honor: Tommy, the leader of the gang of boys; and Gimpty, an out-of-work and slightly crippled architect who dreams of building decent housing for the poor. And in each generational group, the honorable character is opposed by a dishonorable one: the malign Spit among the boys; and Baby-Face Martin, a gangster with a reward on his head who has returned to the "old neighborhood" to try to reconnect with both his mother and an old love, among the adults. In each generational group, this honor is tested, and the highly ambiguous results reveal the difficulty, if not impossibility, of escaping poverty with one's honor in tact. Tommy eventually forgoes vengeance on Spit for the latter's selling him out to the authorities for the promise of cash, and turns himself in. Gimpty, on the other hand, resolves his difficulties by collecting reward money for providing information that leads to the police's killing of Baby-Face, his childhood friend. At play's end, the parallel plots come together when Gimpty plans to marry Drina (Tommy's sister and guardian), and use his reward money to get Tommy the best lawyer money can buy – a "happy" ending, but a morally ambiguous one given the play's themes of honor and the corrupting influence of money.

From beginning to end, the world of the play is one in which nearly all relations between people involve economic transactions. The gang of boys, Kingsley is careful to show, gain their sense that everything in life has a price from adults. Early in the first act, this is made clear when Angel – the most innocent member of Tommy's gang – cannot produce information sought by Baby-Face Martin's goon and then asks for money. The goon's reply, "Nuttin' fer nuttin," characterizes the life of the play's characters more succinctly than any other single line (100). The sickly boy T.B has learned a similar lesson in reform school: he explains in Act II that there, inmates get "slop" to eat "unless dey git some dough tuh smeah' da jailies wid" (150).

The boys clearly take lessons like these to heart. While on one level they share a degree of camaraderie not seen among any of the adult characters in the play, as they spend their days swimming in the polluted waters of the East River, hatching plots to acquire money or food, and taunting their rich neighbors, their relations are also characterized by a certain lack of trust that is repeatedly associated in the play with economic relations. Nothing is freely given. When Milty, a new boy, wants to enter their gang, he must pay cash to the gang leader, Tommy. Tommy obviously likes and respects Milty; but business is business, and the payment must be made (95). When Spit steals a "boy-scout knife" from Angel, Tommy intervenes and returns the knife to its rightful owner. But even this seemingly generous act becomes part of an economic transaction, through Tommy's pointed remark to Angel: "Don' say I nevuh gave yuh nuttin!" (94). The comment seems to make Tommy's action less the giving of a gift than the establishing of credit to be called in at some later date. Add to these instances the nearly constant accusations that one or another of the boys is "holding out" by not sharing some real or imagined bit of cash, and the instances where one boy physically searches another for money, and it becomes clear that money, on one level, functions naturalistically in this play as a force that has "corrupted" the boys' otherwise easy-going and "innocent" relations. The boys' "fall" from innocence into experience is likewise a fall into the economic.

While this corrupting aspect of money seems clearly meant to shock the play's 1935 audience by showing the morally crippling effects of capitalism, especially on the young, Kingsley wants to present another side to the representation of money in this play. When, in the next act, Tommy tries to use the credit he established earlier by asking to borrow Angel's knife, the latter refuses to lend it. When the situation threatens to become violent, Milty, the new boy who bought his way into the gang, solves the problem by *buying* the knife from Angel and then *giving* it to Tommy. This one gratuitous act is almost more than Tommy can process. "Yuh mean yuh givin' it tuh me?" asks Tommy in disbelief (122). Tommy's surprise at the very idea of a gift speaks much about the brutally calculating nature of the boys' world. And when Milty shrugs off Tommy's appreciation, insisting, "dat's nuttin,'" Tommy insists "dat's a whole lot" (122-23). Aside from the play's concluding scene, where Tommy declines to punish Spit for betraying him, this gift-giving represents the sole episode in the play where one of the boys gives something to another without demanding something in return. Yet this gift is only made possible through an economic transaction – Milty's buying the knife from Angel. In this instance, Kingsley seems to want to show that the fact that everything in the boys' world has a price is not necessarily incompatible with selfless and altruistic acts between people. In fact, Milty's ability to buy the knife seems to make the violence, threatened or real, that normally characterizes the way the boys get what they want unnecessary. Similarly, Milty's buying his way into Tommy's gang brings Milty and Tommy together and avoids Milty's being harassed by the boys, while in another sense reducing that coming-together to a business transaction.

In *The Philosophy of Money* Simmel locates several of the paradoxes Kingsley would explore in *Dead End* as both the symbolic content and practical consequence of money. In a money economy, notes Simmel, a certain coolness or objectivity must exist if goods are to acquire *prices,* which presuppose their being bought or sold in the marketplace rather than simply taken at will. For Simmel, this coolness represents the distance that allows the individual human subject to perceive an objective, "real" world existing outside his own subjective consciousness. Economic exchange is "the representative of the distance between subject and object which transforms subjective feelings into objective valuation" (90). Money thus becomes a symbol of both desire and the necessary cooling of desire. Simmel's analysis offers insight into the paradoxical nature of money in the world of the children of *Dead End.* While in one sense money represents a certain coldness or distance in the relations of each boy to the other – a kind of loss of innocence – in another sense Kingsley seems to want to show that money facilitates social freedom and provides an alternative to violence and theft.

But these benefits come at a cost. In the money-centered world of *Dead End,* where all relations take on the properties of economic relations between commodities, identity emerges as a major problem. One way this is manifest is a near-constant suspicion and mistrust among the characters. No one's identity can be certain; no one's word can be trusted. When Tommy, near the end of the play, threatens to hurt Angel if the latter reveals his plans to catch Spit, Angel protests, "Aw, Tommy, yuh know me . . . yuh know me!" But this is not good enough: Tommy repeats his threat and Angel repeats his plea (153). Similarly, when Tommy's older sister Drina pleads to Mr. Griswald to accept Tommy's word and not press charges for the boy's having injured him with a knife, Griswald refuses:

> Drina: But you heard him. He swore he wouldn't ever do it again.
> Griswald: I'm afraid I can't believe that. (163)

The newspapers, we are reminded at least twice, cannot be trusted either: "I'm not here," Martin tells Gimpty, "I'm out West. Read da papers" (102); and later, Francey tells Martin, "They said yuh wuz out aroun' Coloradah—th'noospapuhs!" (138).

The play's association of money with an arbitrary relationship between appearance and reality finds its most powerful and uncanny manifestation in the gangster Baby-Face Martin. Appearing in the first act with a surgically altered face, dyed hair, and an assumed name, he is also a man, we are told in the stage directions, *"given to sudden volcanic violences that come and are gone in a breath"* (90). This frightening volatility and inconstancy characterize most of his interactions with other characters throughout the play. Related to his own lack of a stable identity is Martin's difficulty recognizing anyone else. It takes Gimpty a few lines in the first act to jog Martin's memory: "Don't you remember me? . . . I'm Gimpty . . . Remember? . . . We were kids here. Don't you remember?" (100). In this encounter, Martin's failure to see contrasts sharply with Gimpty's recognition of Martin, despite the gangster's radically altered physical appearance. Martin, of course, doesn't want to be recognized and insists, "I ain't Martin, you bastard!" and, a few lines later, "My name's Johnson. Git it? Johnson" (100). In this play, Martin is a walking manifestation of the radical break between appearance and essence, face value and material value represented by money.

Martin's calling Gimpty a "bastard" is interesting in that it questions Gimpty's origins and identity. But of course, the irony is that it is Martin who is in an important sense a bastard, rejected as he is by his own mother in the second act. Martin's failed attempt to reconnect with his mother begins with a failure of recognition (Martin: "It's me. *No recognition.* I had my face fixed"[127]) and ends with a *refusal* to recognize: "Don't call me Mom!" responds Martin's mother, "Yuh ain't no son of mine" and later "Why don't yuh leave me ferget yuh?"(127). Martin's mother's failure to either visually or existentially recognize Martin as her son is a powerful instance of the play's association of money with monstrosity. Denied as he is by his own mother, the "self-made" and cosmetically transformed Martin becomes disturbingly self-generating: he bears no discernable trace of his origins and appears to have been bred out of his own "barren" metal. Faced with this dilemma, Martin ironically and tragically tries to reconnect with his mother via the very medium that marks his separation, as he tries to trade money for his mother's love; but Mrs. Martin refuses to take what she calls his "blood money" (128).

"Blood money" is an interesting idea given the play's exploration of money's "neutrality" or "lack of character." The notion that money can carry a moral taint as a result of the way in which it was earned seems to run counter to the very idea of money as elaborated by thinkers like Simmel and Shell. The idea of blood money denies money's lack of character, and therefore seems to represent what a postmodern perspective might view as the repression of money. In other words, if it is the alienating and neutralizing effects of money that one is bothered by, then the notion of money that takes on the character of its user can be seen as comforting. But interestingly, just a few lines earlier, Martin's mother invokes just those qualities of money her later comment will deny, when she tells her son to leave and "not come back like a bad penny!" (128). On one level, Martin's mother's words indicate the gangster's physical change by comparing him to counterfeit money – he appears to be what he is in fact not. There is also an obvious moral connotation in her use of "bad," reflecting her disgust at Martin's degraded humanity. At closer inspection however, it seems clear that the line expresses horror not at the commodification of Martin, but just the opposite: Martin's mother blames her son for not *fully* becoming a commodity. He has "come back" to his mother, has refused to be "spent" the way a bad (i.e. counterfeit) penny might come back to its would-be spender. On this level, what is counterfeit or false about Martin is not the persona he has adopted; what is counterfeit is his trying to be again what he once was. As money and nothing else, Baby-Face in no way reflects morally on his mother. If she lets her son reconnect with her on what she perceives as a more fundamental level, she is forced to share the blame in what he has become. This is dramatized in the play by her *"clutching her stomach,"* and crying "in here! Kickin'! That's where you come from. God! I ought to be cut open fer givin' yuh life . . . murderer!!!" (128). Rather than live with this guilt, Mrs. Martin seeks the only comfort available to her in what Simmel calls the distanced or "cool" relations that result from the commodification of life and that find their most powerful symbol in money. Yet the horrifying spectacle of Martin's rejection by his mother surely problematizes the play's tendency toward a rather pragmatic view of the morality of money relations.

Money plays a similarly important role in Martin's next failed attempt to reconnect with his past. Like the encounter between Martin and his mother, this one also begins with a failure of recognition. In the second act, Martin manages to locate his old lover Francey, but refuses to see what is obvious to both the audience and other characters in the play: that she has become a diseased prostitute. Kingsley's stage directions tell us Francey is *"an obvious whore of the lowest class, wearing her timeless profession defiantly"*; yet Martin refuses to see and is puzzled by

Francey's obvious embarrassment, until, finally, the stage directions tell us he *"sees her. The nostalgic dream is finished. His lips begin to curl in disgust"* (139). When Martin asks Francey why she didn't get a job or even "starve' rather than become a prostitute, Francey asks him why *he* didn't do the same; yet Martin seems oblivious to the extent to which he has sold himself just like Francey (140).

As it did in the confrontation between Martin and his mother, in this one between Martin and Francey once again money figures paradoxically as that which creates distance between characters, and, tragically, as the only available means for overcoming that distance. Francey's turning herself into a commodity has led to her illness. Now, *"clutching at hope,"* she suggests that perhaps Martin's money can pay for a doctor to make her healthy again. But this time it is Martin who is more pessimistic about the powers of money. Still, Francey's eyes are *"glued to the money"* in Martin's hand, and her attempts to wheedle more and more out of him leave him ever more disgusted (140).

A version of the self-made man, Martin has lived by his own rules. He justifies his life of crime to Gimpty in the first act, explaining that he couldn't wait around "fer Santa Claus tuh take care a me" and had to act (102). And he has made a kind of success of himself. But in being *self-made,* he trades a "deeper" sense of identity, of place (the "old neighborhood"), and of connection with others (Francey and his mother) for money. When Gimpty expresses disapproval of what Martin has done to earn his money, Martin answers by rattling off the prices of various items of expensive clothing he is wearing (103). In Kingsley's moral equation, the freedom from his past, the overcoming of his environment Martin has gained has come at the cost of his own humanity, and at play's end the transition from human being to commodity is complete when Gimpty cashes in on the reward money for helping to kill Martin. The complete erasure of Martin's identity, the total transformation from man into monster is dramatized at the end of the second act as a medical intern called to the scene remarks, "They certainly did a job on him! Nothing left to look at but chopped meat" (145). Hal Foster reads the prominence of "images of corporeal fragmentation" in American literature of the thirties as evidence of an anxiety over "the becoming machine and/or commodity of the body" (qtd. in Solomon 14). The description certainly fits the character of Baby-Face Martin, who is both commodity and (through his plastic surgery) a piece of technology. Arriving on the scene, Mulligan the police officer reads off Martin's height, weight, and marital status, and remarks with admiration on Martin's diamond ring and "roll of bills" (145). The man who bought his way out of the "dead end" of the ghetto ends up as cash and *nothing else.*

The polar opposite of the calculating, pragmatic Martin, Pete Gimpty, the out-of-work architect whose lame leg symbolizes his inability to escape the ghetto, is (at the beginning of the play) the idealist almost to the point of caricature. If Martin personifies a modernist, commodified present irrevocably cut off from the past, Gimpty conversely seems oblivious to present realities and lives entirely in recollections of the past and utopian plans for the future – the latter represented by his architectural drawings for housing that, he seems to believe, will never be built. Kingsley's stage directions describe Gimpty as a *"sensitive-faced young man"* with a drawing board in his lap. They also tell us, *"Occasionally he will work feverishly . . . , then he will let the pencil droop, and stare out over the river with deep-set eyes, dream-laden, moody"* (86). In a way Gimpty's distractedness from present reality allows him to see through what deceives others: he recognizes Martin despite the gangster's greatly changed appearance, explaining the recognition by the fact that he knew Martin as a child (155). On the other hand, Gimpty's refusal (or inability) to live in the present leaves him oblivious, most of the time, to Drina's obvious attraction to him and to the downward moral spiral of the kids from the neighborhood.

Once he recognizes him, Martin remembers Gimpty as an honorable and trustworthy kid (100). And the difference between Gimpty's idealism and Martin's pragmatism is demonstrated in at least two scenes. In the first act Martin sneeringly points out that Gimpty, who followed society's rules for achieving success by getting an education and learning a profession, is on home relief while Martin got rich by taking what he wanted and breaking the rules (102-103). In the second act, Gimpty strongly objects to the advice Martin gives to the gang of boys regarding how to conduct a fight with a rival gang: "when yuh fight, dee idee is tuh win. It don' cut no ice how" and "If yuh wanna win, yuh gotta make up yer own rules, see?" (121).

In the course of the play, the idealism Kingsley is careful to associate with Gimpty receives a series of blows, and money figures in each. The first blow comes in the form of Baby-Face Martin, whose moral pragmatism and materialism seem to have provided a path out of the same ghetto that traps Gimpty. The next blow comes in the form of a failed relationship. Gimpty is in love with Kay, an upwardly mobile resident of the luxury high-rise building that towers over Gimpty's "old neighborhood." But Kay soon recognizes that she is not willing to give up money and the life it makes possible to marry Gimpty, and instead will marry the wealthy Jack Hilton, whom she does not love. She explains to Gimpty, "I've known what it means to scrimp and worry and never be sure from one minute to the next. I've had enough of that." When Gimpty suggests that living without love is "not living at all," Kay answers that she "can do without" love (113). A moment later, prodded by Gimpty, Kay claims she doesn't really mean this. But her meaning is clear in her decision ultimately not to be with Gimpty.[5] Kay explains to Gimpty in the second act, "I could do this. I could go and live with you and be happy . . . and then when poverty comes . . . . I'd leave you and go back to Jack." Gimpty is hurt, but thanks Kay for helping him see "clearly" – that is, see beyond his earlier idealism regarding money (156).

The culmination of Gimpty's degraded idealism is his decision to turn Martin in and collect the reward money. In the second act, the inept police officer Mulligan warns Gimpty that whoever goes after Martin is taking a big chance. Gimpty responds, "you can't live forever" – words that clearly echo Martin's philosophy of taking your chances and getting what you can (136). By the third act, once Martin is dead and Gimpty is set to receive the reward money, the latter expresses regret at the lack of honor of turning a childhood friend in to the police, though Kay insists it "had to be done" and reminds Gimpty that he can now help his mother and "live decently" (156). Presumably, Gimpty may also now turn some of his architectural drawings of low-income housing into real structures. He may be having occasional regrets, but Gimpty by play's end has certainly adopted a more pragmatic view regarding the necessity of money and the too-high cost of honor.

Not surprisingly, the less moral distance there is between Gimpty and the fragmented, commodified persona that is Baby-Face Martin, the more riddled is Gimpty with doubt concerning identity – his own as well as others'. Early in the first act, these doubts are focused on Martin. Gimpty explains that when he would read newspaper stories about Martin's exploits, which include killing eight men, he "never could quite believe" it was the same person he had known as a child (102). But as the play progresses, there is an obvious correlation between Gimpty's growing acceptance of the importance of money and his growing existential doubt, illustrating once again the association of money with what Simmel called a "lack of character." In the second act, Gimpty, having just lost Kay because of a lack of funds, suggests to Drina that she should follow her friends' lead and seek a rich man to marry. When Drina remarks that this "doesn't sound like" Gimpty, the latter asks, "How do you know what goes on inside of me?" (134). As money is the site of the break between "material" and "intellectual currency," it is associated repeatedly in *Dead End* with the inability to discern from the "outside" what exists on the "inside" of anyone.

The existential uncertainty represented by money and implied by Gimpty's question pervades the play generally, but is manifested in a particularly subtle yet powerful manner through the play's meta-dramatic elements. These include several scenes in which characters – usually members of Tommy's gang – engage in what theorist Richard Hornby calls "role-playing within the role," an activity that, Hornby points out, "exposes the very nature of role itself," thus "reminding us that all human roles are relative, that identities are learned rather than innate"(72). In three instances, all within the third act, the boys play-act, assuming the successive roles of gangsters, rich party-goers, and a cruise liner (148, 157). Another meta-dramatic element is Kingsley's use of allegorical names for the characters (Gimpty, who is lame; T.B., who has tuberculosis; and Baby-Face, who has a new face, are but three examples). On the one hand, these allegorical names disrupt the realism of the play by foregrounding the characters *as characters,* by reminding us that we are watching a performance of reality and not reality. On the other hand, the allegorical names seem to reinforce the positivist outlook at the heart of realism, for in a sense the signs that are the characters' names do seem to reflect the "essence" of the characters. A similarly complicated metadramatic element of *Dead End* is the decentering, almost too realistic set by Norman Bel Geddes. At the play's premiere, Joseph Wood Krutch noted the strangeness of Bel Geddes' "unusually elaborate" set, which turned the stage apron into a "very realistic dock front" that placed the audience "somewhere in the East River" of New York City. "Once one has gotten over the fear of seeing a tugboat come down the aisle or of finding a melon rind in one's lap it is all very striking," noted Krutch (57). Bel Geddes' set, the allegorical names of the characters, and the instances of role-playing within dramatic roles work in concert to complicate the "realism" of the play, thus amplifying Gimpty's question about how we may know who anyone is "on the inside."

These same questions regarding identity that trouble Gimpty also plague Tommy and the rest of the boys throughout the play. Clearly troubled by the radical uncertainty of a world where everything and everyone is for sale, the boys occasionally try to find a way to distinguish true from false and good from bad. One such instance occurs in the beginning of the first act. Spit, the stage directions tell us, *"makes a swipe"* at Dippy, the most innocent of the boys. Then, enforcing some understood rule, Spit insists he now gets to hit Dippy twice because the latter flinched at the swipe. When Dippy insists he did not flinch, the boys agree to "choose fer it" in order to divine the truth (87). When Dippy wins the first throw, he declares, "See? Cheatin' shows!" (88). But then Spit, who holds no such faith in moral transparency, wins the next two throws and answers Dippy: "Cheatin' shows? Yeah. Boy, ahl knock yuh fer a loop!"(88). What may seem at first glance like an insignificant moment in the play has great significance for the play's treatment of money. Dippy's hope that Spit's dishonesty would be revealed through the game of "choosing for it" is the expression of a longing for a moral transparency not to be found in the world of the play. The lying Spit – a character who later turns Tommy in for cash – represents the increasingly arbitrary relation between surface and meaning, material and essence represented by money. Dippy attempts to deny this tendency by choosing to believe that, essentially, "the truth will out" in the manner of a medieval joust. These are essentially the same two views held by the adult characters Gimpty and Martin at the beginning of the pay.

Struggling between these two views of the world is the character of Tommy. Repeatedly in the play we see less powerful members of the gang appeal successfully to Tommy's sense of honor and fairness. Usually, this involves preventing Spit from taking unfair advantage of one of them. Even in the incident that gets him into serious trouble – the beating of the wealthy and arrogant young Griswald boy that leads to the unpremeditated stabbing of the boy's politically connected father – Tommy evinces a kind of fair play, as we learn that each of the boys, Tommy included, underwent a similar beating as a kind of initiation when they first moved to the neighborhood. We even witness such an initiation performed on Milty, who is later accepted into the gang.

The struggle Tommy enters into in this play finally comes down to one between the two extremes represented by Dippy and Spit in the "cheatin' shows" episode, and by Gimpty and Martin among the adult characters. Tommy struggles against what is symbolically represented by money in this play: the absence of a firm ground for identity, the gulf between appearance and reality. When Spit first tells a policeman that it was Tommy who stabbed Mr. Griswald, and then demonstrates that he is willing to lead the police right to Tommy in exchange for a monetary reward, Tommy plans to give Spit the "Mark a de squealuh" by creating a permanent scar on Spit's face, thus ensuring that Spit's "outside" reflects his "inside" – that "cheatin' shows" (153). Spit's sin is that he would sell Tommy out for money. Tommy's plan to "mark" Spit in this way evinces the former's intense longing for an answer to the question posed by Gimpty: how does anyone know what goes on inside anyone else in a world where everyone and everything is for sale? The existential uncertainty represented by the shape-changing, commodified persona that is Baby-Face Martin is precisely what Tommy is trying to put an end to when he tries to "mark" Spit. The irony is that Tommy's violent act, one that Gimpty and Drina see as likely to send him on a path toward a life like that of Baby-Face Martin, is actually a striking out *against* what Martin represents: Tommy would essentially place material and intellectual currency back in sync with one another, reversing the tendency represented by money.

This irony is deepened by the fact that in pleading with Tommy, in the climactic scene of the play, *not* to mark Spit, Gimpty and Drina advise Tommy to do, in a sense, the *dishonorable* thing. And unsurprisingly, at the heart of this decision is money. First Spit, true to form, tries to buy his freedom by offering Tommy all sorts of goods, and cash, in return for letting him go. When Tommy refuses to be bought, Gimpty first asks Tommy to hand him the knife and then, incredibly, hits on a new idea: "Sell it to me! I'll buy it from you!" (159). Gimpty's attempt to buy the knife from Tommy – an utterly bizarre act unless we consider the thematic importance of money in this play – shows the former's total blindness regarding what it is that Tommy is fighting against: the replacement of all values with economic values, the moral de-valuation of everything that seems to accompany the monetary valuation of everything. Once Tommy finally hands the knife to his sister Drina, Gimpty unveils his plan: he'll use the reward money he earned by turning in Martin to buy Tommy "the best lawyer in this city," thereby helping Tommy to avoid the poisonous atmosphere of reform school, which Gimpty feels would likely turn the boy into another Baby-Face Martin (165).

Of course, Gimpty is right to urge Tommy to forego vengeance and thereby avoid the path of Baby-Face. Through Gimpty's using his reward money to save Tommy, the play attempts ultimately to "redeem" money in the moral sense. The very characteristic of money that signifies alienation among the characters is ultimately what makes Gimpty's act possible: what Simmel calls money's "neutrality" or "lack of character." The same cash can be used to both good and bad ends, and the morality of either the human actors or their actions does not attach to that money. Ultimately, for Gimpty, there is no "blood money," nor are there any "bad pennies." At the same time, the life (and the death) of Baby-Face Martin stand as markers of the degraded humanity that seems to accompany the replacement of human values by economic ones, which tends to problematize Gimpty's embracing of money at play's end as the only available solution to the problems money has created.

Brenda Murphy has described *Dead End* and other American "realist" plays of the thirties as combining a traditionally naturalistic view of "outside"/environmental forces as determinative of character with an infusion of Freudian psychology (*American Realism* 61). In *Dead End,* money exists symbolically at the intersection of these two philosophical and aesthetic worldviews. Gimpty's mother's notion of "blood money" (or money that is not money, that does not possess what Simmel calls money's "neutrality" or "lack of character") may be seen as an instance of the repression of money at the heart of literary naturalism. Spit's need to believe that "cheatin' shows," and Tommy's desperate desire to place an outward "mark" on Spit to correspond to his "inward" state, are similar attempts to repress the arbitrary relation of appearance to essence symbolized in the play by money.

Ultimately, however, Kingsley's play seems to reject the notion of a "natural" and "stable" value in favor of a view that accepts both the role of money as a difficult but necessary element in American life and the similar role of signification in that life, symbolized by the new American family that emerges at play's end: Gimpty, Drina, and young Tommy, a "nuclear family" made possible by a combination of Drina's love, Gimpty's moral pragmatism, Tommy's acceptance of a world where everything (and everyone) is for sale, and the best lawyer money can buy.

CHAPTER THREE

"THE JUNGLE IS DARK AND FULL OF DIAMONDS": NATURAL VALUE AND REALITY TESTING IN MILLER'S *DEATH OF A SALESMAN*

By 1949, when Arthur Miller's seminal play opened at the Morosco Theatre on Broadway, the economy had recovered from the crash of 1929, but what Miller called the "hypocrisies" exposed by the Depression had become both deeper and more widespread as the post-war industrial boom and the explosion of the advertising and public relations industries worked feverishly to create the commodified, hyper-mediated world we live in today. In investigating the disturbing ubiquity of "business" values, the replacement of all values with economic ones, and the inability to think of oneself other than as commodity, Miller's masterpiece would seem to reevaluate the compromise that ended Kingsley's play, where another family (the boy Tommy, his older sister Drina, and the adult Pete Gimpty) trade their idealism for a moral pragmatism that accepts and even tries to find use for the objectifying, alienating characteristics of an advanced money economy. At the same time, like *Dead End,* Miller's play certainly complicates the logic of naturalism, where all is seen as *either* "real" or mimetic, "natural" value or worthless imitation. The initial stage directions already point to the play's complication of this logic when they describe the Loman house as "*a dream rising out of reality*" (338). Yet the aspect of the play that most powerfully complicates this distinction is ultimately the figure of the salesman himself.

In his critical examination of cultural representations of the traveling salesman from the first half of the twentieth century, Timothy Spears finds him "occupying a rather nebulous territory that separated an older America from a newer one." In works by Edna Ferber, George Horace Lattimore, Sherwood Anderson, and Willa Cather, the salesman or "commercial traveler" plays the role of "cultural middleman," figuring "not only as a representative of modern business success but also as a remnant of the past" (Spears 5). Spears sees the early twentieth-century salesman's simultaneously representing the past and the future as a locally historical phenomenon, caught as he is between "an older, 'residual' face-to-face marketplace" and "an 'emergent' corporate economy" that threatens to replace him with print advertising (7). But the ambivalence toward the past and the future Spears identifies as peculiar to the nineteenth-century traveling salesman represents a phenomenon that did not disappear from our cultural landscape with the passing of this version of the commercial traveler. In fact, the salesman's paradoxical relation to time is intimately related to other paradoxes – the tangled distinction between talk and action, change and stasis, the mechanical and the organic, the city and the country – that we all live to an ever-increasing degree in what has become, to quote the title of Earl Shorris's study, a "Nation of Salesmen."

One of the most salient aspects of *Death of a Salesman,* and one that foreshadows a concern of later works in this study, is the play's exploration of the distinction between saying and doing, talk and action. Often taken as evidence of what Richard Hofstadter, in *Anti-Intellectualism in American Life,* famously delineated as the business world's general hostility toward intellectuals and almost religious dedication to "practicality," the American businessman, at least in the twentieth century, appears on the literary and cultural scene as a self-described "man of action" with no time for "idle talk." Miller's illiterate businessman father, about whom the author seems often conflicted, may have furnished the playwright with an early example of business's bifurcation of "talk" and "action." Early in his autobiography, however, Miller illustrates this tendency in his description of his maternal grandfather. A formidable businessman rather obsessed with his physical appearance, Louis Barnett, according to Miller, never uttered "a word . . . that might have some attachment to a thought" or indeed "a sound that was not immediately useful or a mere greeting or a goodbye." He had "a tendency to direct action" evidenced both by his preference for physical violence over words when communicating with union organizers in his employ and by his belief that Franklin Roosevelt should not be allowed to run for President of the United States against Hoover "because Roosevelt had never run a business" *(Timebends* 5). While Miller's grandfather's instrumentalist conception of language has long been associated with businessmen generally, the salesman, in particular, has reason to possess a somewhat more complicated attitude toward language. The fact that the salesman, more than any other businessman, makes his living *by talking* leads to a profound ambivalence toward language that complicates the distinction between language and action that business rhetoric would otherwise maintain. The salesman, in Miller's play, represents at once a heightened understanding of the dialectical inseparability of "talk" and "action" and a deep anxiety caused by this knowledge.

The very insistence on a hard distinction between talk and action reveals an anxiety over the unavoidable ambiguity and misdirection of language. It has become axiomatic that Willy Loman mistakes saying for doing; a look at the attitudes toward the spoken word of the major characters in the play, however, reveals something more complex. Linda clearly sees Willy's excessive "saying" as indicative of a lack of doing: as she explains to Biff and Happy, "Instead of walking he talks now" (57). In Linda's formulation, language (Willy's "talking") denotes the absence of reality – it *takes the place of* action. It is true that at times Willy seems to possess an almost boundless faith in the ability of one's words to have a real impact on the world, merely through their utterance. At the same time, however, Willy recognizes his profuse talking as a liability. Searching for reasons for his failure at sales, Willy tells Linda, "I don't know why --I can't stop myself --I talk too much" (37). In fact at other times in the play Willy tries his best to limit or outright prevent the talk of other characters in the play. After the first memory-scene involving the "Woman" Willy has a sexual affair with in Boston, the stage directions tell us that Willy attempts to silence Linda by *"put[ting his] hand gently over her mouth"* (40). A moment later, unwilling to face unpleasant truths about Biff, he tells first Bernard and then Linda to "Shut up!" (40). Later in the first act, he commands Linda, "Don't talk any more" (68). The situation is clearly more complicated than Willy's simply mistaking "talk" for "action." Rather, Willy seems to glean something about the slipperiness of this very distinction, and tries to control reality through controlling speech. Willy's complicated attitude toward "talk" and its relation to "action" is intimately related to his profession. The salesman by definition complicates any easy distinction between saying and doing. He engages in speech that is what philosopher John L. Austin has called "performative" – he performs actions through the uttering of words, thus complicating the distinction between the symbolic and the real (5).

Contrasted with the garrulous Willy is Charley, whose very existence provides a constant critique of Willy's equation of business success with a certain type of speaking. Described in the stage directions as *"laconic"* and *"slow of speech,"* Charley seems wholly lacking in the qualities Willy associates with business success; yet it is Charley and not Willy who makes a modest success in business (41). Willy even tells Linda, in a moment of self-doubt, that unlike himself, Charley is "respected" because he is "a man of few words" (37). And like Linda, Charley seems to appreciate doing over saying. When Willy shows surprise that Bernard is about to argue a case in front of the Supreme Court and yet "didn't even mention it" in his conversation with Willy, Charley replies, "He don't have to [mention it,] he's gonna do it," echoing the view of language expressed in Linda's comment – as that which *replaces* reality, or that which denotes its absence: one talks *instead of* walking (95).

Less obvious perhaps than Charley's facile distinction between talk and action is the fact that his comment about Bernard at the same time inadvertently equates speech (arguing in front of the Supreme Court) with *doing.* It is an irony lost to most critics of the play that Bernard – the character who would correct Biff's mistaking of language for action by telling him that writing the words "University of Virginia" on his shoes will not lead to his going there (32)– emerges by the end of the play as one who makes his living by using language to affect reality. In fact the lawyer's speech shares much with the salesman's: both are meant to persuade; both rely heavily on extra-verbal factors such as appearance, intonation, and body language; both are essentially performative.

By 1951, just two years after *Salesman* opened in New York, C. Wright Mills saw increasingly little difference between most lawyers and other businessmen. He noted that while the popular image of lawyers has always been rather ambiguous, by the mid-twentieth century a shift occurs whereby "the public has become for the lawyer what the public has been for the lawyer's chief client [the large corporations] – an object of profit rather than of obligation" (122). This new lawyer emerging in the first half of the twentieth century is a "groomed personality" and "a businessman himself, a proprietor of high acumen, good training, many contacts, and sound judgment" (Mills 123). "The top men" in law firms are "chosen as are film stars, for their glamour" (124). Mills' portrait of the emerging twentieth-century lawyer has him as a kind of morally sanctioned confidence man, a paid persuader who wraps his ethically questionable practices in the cloak of professionalism as he climbs the social and economic ladder.

In Miller's play, "contacts" and image seem as important to the lawyer Bernard's success as they would be to any salesman's: we are told he is to play tennis at the home of a friend who has his own courts (which both impresses Willy greatly and seems to imply that the football-playing Biff, rather than choosing the wrong values, merely chose the wrong sport), and his waiting with valise in hand for a train resembles in important respects a popular image of the salesman (the first image in the play is the salesman Willy entering with his "sample cases"). He is even told by his father to "Knock 'em dead," one of Willy's favorite trite phrases to describe selling (95). This coupled with the contradictory and clichéed advice he offers Willy – "If at first you don't succeed . . ." followed by "sometimes, Willy, it's better for a man just to walk away" – complicates Christopher Bigsby's reading of Bernard and Charley as evidence that "a full-hearted commitment to capitalism is not incompatible with humane values" (Miller 95, Bigsby 84). The characters demonstrate, rather, the disturbing ubiquity of salesmanship in twentieth-century America. Critics like Bigsby, Gardner, and Jordan Miller seem to miss some of the play's complexity when they view Bernard's success as a vindication of capitalist values. It is, after all, the depersonalized, manipulative nature of business relationships – not their purported ability to make one "successful" – that is being critiqued here.

Willy's brother Ben complicates the distinction between talk and action even further, and powerfully associates that complication with money. Like Charley, Ben seems to label as impotent Willy's brand of "talk," preferring things of value you can "feel with the hand" over what he seems to view as Willy's pie-in-the-sky rambling (126). In this sense Ben's view of language is in accord with Linda's and Charley's, viewing it as absence, as the opposite of "concrete" reality. But Ben also appreciates (and possibly fears) the power of effective "talk" of the sort Bernard is eventually engaged in as an attorney. Attempting to enlist Willy in his Alaska adventures, Ben clearly recognizes no place in his business enterprises for "talk" of either sort: "You've got a new continent at your doorstep, William. Get out of these cities, they're full of talk and time payments and courts of law. Screw on your fists and you can fight for a fortune up there" (359). Ben's aversion to "talk and time payments and courts of law" is unsurprising considering the lawless land-grabs and exploitative labor practices we assume he is pursuing in Africa and Alaska. In Ben's rhetoric, language denotes both power and its absence: the ineffective "talk" of Willy represents a failure to act, while the effective "talk" of courts of law threatens to subject his business practices to ethical and legal analysis.

At the same time, Ben is a sophisticated user of language in his own right. If Ben's philosophy of "screwing on one's fists" and fighting for "a fortune" represents in this play the ruthless "realities" of capitalism, Ben is adept at obfuscating those realities when it suits him. Asked by Willy for the "secret" of his success, Ben replies each time with a carefully edited rags-to-riches narrative: "when I was seventeen I walked into the jungle, and when I was twenty-one I walked out. *(He laughs.)* And by God I was rich" (349). The violence and deceit which, as we learn from his rough play with Biff,[6] were essential to Ben's acquiring his fortune in "the jungle" are here omitted, with the phrase "by God" hinting at both an explanation of and justification for Ben's wealth.[7] Ben's use of "God" to obfuscate the realities of capitalism and justify the acquisition of wealth after the fact has many precedents, from the American concept of "manifest destiny" to J.P. Morgan's apocryphal remark, in answer to a small child who asked why he had so much money while the child's family did not, that God wanted Morgan to be rich. Ben clearly knows how to weave a narrative that places his own success in the best light, demonstrating that despite his statements to the contrary, "talk" is an essential part of his "action."

If Ben is, as Willy calls him, "success incarnate," then he also represents Willy's repressed knowledge of the rather unpleasant exigencies of achieving such success. But Willy's repression of the violence and aggression represented by Ben only leads to this violence resurfacing elsewhere in Willy's words and actions. In the first "memory scene" of Act I Willy imparts his Frank Capra-like business philosophy to Biff and Happy: "Be liked and you will never want" (345). But the naivete of this outlook is immediately underscored by the violent sales metaphors employed by Willy and Biff in the lines just following:

> BIFF: Did you knock them dead, Pop?
> WILLY: Knocked 'em cold in Providence, slaughtered 'em in Boston. (345)

Even more telling is Willy's description of "business" in a conversation with Ben later in the same act: "Business is bad, it's murderous. But not for me, of course" (350). Ostensibly yet another simultaneous confession and denial of Willy's own failings as a salesman, this statement also reads as a moral judgment on the type of "business" Ben engages in and an attempt by Willy to separate his sort of "business" from his brother's. As such the statement seems to invite the response that *all* business is murderous to a greater or lesser extent.

Even more significantly, the violent descriptions of business underscore the violence implicit in the depersonalized, manipulative relations that characterize the commodified life of the salesman and the business world generally – one in which people are viewed as "prospects," as means to an end rather than ends in themselves, where their resistance must be overcome – where, as Guy Oakes explains in a 1990 study of the insurance salesman, "[e]veryone is employed as a tool for maximizing sales": "The agent is governed by an instrumental conception of rationality the object of which is to transform everyone, including the agent, into an effective means for the realization of sales objectives that are regarded as ultimate and unquestionable axioms" (38). Where the salesman's vitality depends on the "closing" of the prospect, relations between salesman and prospect take on the quality of a life-and-death struggle[8]: to succeed, Willy "slaughters" his clients; Charlie's unsuccessful New England salesman "comes back bleedin', they murdered him up there" (Miller 51). Today salesmen still speak of their work in these violent terms. Oakes' study quotes a contemporary insurance salesman who explains that similar language is used in his line of sales: "There are terms like 'Hit em!' That's a common term in insurance. 'I'm gonna hit him again, I'm gonna hit him again.' What he means is, he's gonna pound away at this guy" (Oakes 70).

The violence inherent in the depersonalized, objectifying relations that make up the salesman's world, a violence which Willy would consciously deny, manifests itself not just in Willy's words but in his actions as well, an aspect of Willy's character emphasized in Robert Falls's explosively physical 1999 Broadway revival of *Salesman.* Willy has obvious difficulty controlling his temper, as evidenced by his story of physically assaulting another salesman in response to a perceived insult, by the outburst in Howard Wagner's office that costs him his job, and by his several exchanges with Charley, in which Willy threatens to "rap [him] one" (346, 359, 363). Willy not only passes this violence on to his sons (Biff's "temper" is mentioned several times and Happy fantasizes about "outbox[ing]" his bosses at work) but at certain moments in the play directs this violence *at* his family. In two separate instances Willy threatens to whip Biff (347,370). And interestingly, at the play's opening, Willy almost runs over "a kid" on his aborted sales trip as a result of daydreaming brought on by Biff's recent return home. Repeatedly we can discern barely-concealed feelings of violence toward his own family, as with Willy's dubious remark to Linda that "on the road" he wants "to grab you sometimes and just kiss the life outa you" (346). In these instances the alienation caused by Willy's need to treat all relations as economic ones lead to thinly veiled expressions of aggression toward his family, pointing out the conflicting value systems Willy is attempting to live by --that of a self-reliant business "pioneer" and that of a caring husband and father. And in this regard it must be remembered that two of Willy's role models, his brother Ben and his father, were successful entrepreneurs who effectively abandoned their families.

One of those role modes, Ben, functions in the play as the uncanny manifestation of Willy's deepest anxieties about the distinction between the real and the imaginary, action and talk – the seeming opposites that ultimately come together in money, that object that highlights the arbitrary relation of material value to face value, and that is both "natural" value and signifier. Ben appears in this play as ghost, past memory, and present hallucination at once – a walking example of what Miller wanted to portray in *Salesman* as "past and present concurrently, with neither one ever coming to a stop" *(Timebends* 131). Ben is an ephemeral being who at the same time represents a "hard" value you can "lay your hand on." Ben's repeatedly contrasting the "hard" value of diamonds with Willy's "appointments" represents the obsession with a "natural money" that characterized the debates surrounding the gold standard. A diamond, claims Ben, is "[n]ot like an appointment at all. A diamond is rough and hard to the touch" (134). As an operator of mines who alternately encourages and discourages Willy's turning himself into cash through suicide, Ben at once represents the naturalist obsession with "hard money" and the concomitant fears of an "insubstantial" paper currency. This makes Ben the perfect tormentor of Willy, whose need to believe in a "hard" value is equaled by his fear that such value does not exist. Ben confirms both these tendencies: "The jungle is dark," he tells Willy, playing on his brother's fear of the absence of value in nature, but it is also "full of diamonds" (98). The ephemeral twenty thousand dollars Willy thinks (probably mistakenly) that his suicide would bring to his family is, says Ben, "something one can feel with the hand, it is there" (126). Willy's response shows the depth of his involvement in the logic of naturalism: "Oh, Ben, that's the whole beauty of it! I see it like a diamond, shining in the dark, hard and rough, that I can pick up and touch in my hand. Not like – like an appointment!" (126). Repressing money even as he chases after it, Willy here turns it into hard, "natural" value as opposed to soft currency.

Of the two principal antagonists of the play, Willy and Biff, each has his own reasons to be anxious about money and its philosophical implications. As we learn late in the first act, Willy has recently been denied a salary and put on "straight commission," as Linda tells Biff and Happy, "like a beginner, an unknown" (351). In fact, in an important sense a salesman is a kind of perpetual beginner, and perpetual unknown. For the salesman working for commission, neither past nor future matter. He is worth exactly what he is making in commission *in the present*, and neither past glories nor promises of future potential matter at all. Willy's loss of salary thus amounts to a kind of negating of his past and future. Working for straight commission, Willy is worth only what he is earning in sales now – which, we learn, is nothing. Given the denial of his past with the company and lack of faith in his future potential that the taking of his salary symbolizes, it is not surprising that Willy feels "kind of temporary" about himself (63). His only escape from the painful, commodified present is to reconstruct memories and project into the future – two processes that become impossible when Biff arrives, thus exacerbating the threat Biff poses to Willy's sense of identity. Willy would value himself – and Biff – either by what he imagines they once were, or by what he imagines they could potentially be in the future. In doing so, he belies an anxiety concerning his (and Biff's) valueless-ness in the present.

Simmel's work offers further perspective on Willy's flight from presence to the absence of nostalgia and planning for the future. In *The Philosophy of Money,* Simmel complicates a popular view of the concept of economic value by pointing out that "[o]bjects are not difficult to acquire because they are valuable, but we call those objects valuable that resist our desire to possess them" (66-67). For an object to be valuable, according to Simmel, two things must occur: a human subject must desire the object; and the object must be somewhat removed from the subject – time, space, labor, or some other barrier must stand between the subject and the object. Moreover, both of these factors have an upper and a lower threshold. If an object is too difficult or too easy to acquire, it becomes valueless: if the subject's desire falls to a certain level, the object loses value; if the subject's desire for the object becomes too intense, the *taking* rather than the *buying* of the object may occur, putting an end to economic value.[9]

For a marketplace to function, the desire by human subjects for commodities must exist, but not become overwhelming. A certain coolness or objectivity must exist if commodities are to acquire prices, which presuppose their being bought or sold in the marketplace rather than simply taken at will. At the moment of consumption, when "the opposition between subject and object is effaced," the commodity has no value, and collapses into the subjectivity of the consumer. By this consumerist mentality, value "is only reinstated as contrast, as an object separated from the subject' (66). One result of this is a feeling of alienation on the part of the consumer – an alienation felt even more strongly in a modern capitalist society where products are created not for individual consumers, but for an impersonal "market."

The salesman thrives on this objective coolness between consumer and commodity, even as he works to "warm" this relationship by inserting himself as a human element at the point of purchase and exacerbating the consumer's desire for the commodity. The salesman uses his "personality" – a word often used by Willy Loman as the answer to nearly every problem – in order to overcome the distance between consumer and commodity. In so doing, he turns *himself* into a commodity – he adopts an "objective" distance toward his own personality, *using* it, experiencing it as a means to an end. He alienates himself from himself in order to overcome the alienation felt by the consumer toward products created impersonally for the market, which in turn leads to the consumer's further alienation. This is why Raymond Williams has described Willy Loman as "a man who from selling things has passed to selling himself, and has become, in effect, a commodity which like other commodities will at a certain point be discarded by the laws of the economy" ("Modern Tragic Literature" 15).

Furthermore, the salesman is trained to only recognize value where there is a certain amount of resistance to be overcome. Unsurprisingly, the salesman Happy falls into this mindset when he longs to marry "[s]omebody with character, with resistance" (Miller 25). This helps explain Willy's preference for a physically distant Biff over his son's actual presence. Linda explains that when Biff writes that he's about to visit, Willy is "all smiles, and talks about the future, and – he's just wonderful. And then the closer you seem to come, the more shaky he gets, and then, by the time you get here, he's arguing, and he seems angry at you" (351). In keeping with Willy's preference for saying over doing, language (as absence) over presence, Willy reacts positively to Biff's letters announcing his immanent arrival, but gets increasingly "shaky" as Biff's actual arrival nears. By keeping the present-day reality of Biff at a comfortable distance, Willy is free to reconstruct memories of happier days. These reconstructed memories in turn allow Willy hope for some sort of regeneration – he "talks about the future." Biff's eventual arrival then causes Willy a double loss. First, Willy's false image of Biff dissipates before the genuine specimen. And second, Biff serves as a painful reminder of Willy's adultery – a memory he'd desperately like to forget – and thereby disrupts this entire process of imaginative regeneration. Biff's presence forces Willy to live in the present, which, for interesting reasons, is exactly where Willy most fears being.

According to Simmel, the centrality in people's lives of the money economy leads to a "growing abstractness and artificiality" that reflects an increasing "symbolization," where a more "primary" sense of someone's or something's worth is replaced by an economic (and therefore market-dependent) value, which in turn comes to be represented by money, which in its turn "undergoes a process of increasing symbolization" (as physical money itself becomes less and less substantial, right down to the present day where it is largely electronic) (Poggi 209). Roland Barthes relates this tendency of money to a semiotic shift from "index" to "sign" which he sees as accompanying the historical shift from feudalism to capitalism.

Where once "money 'revealed'; it was an index, it furnished a fact, a cause, it had a nature; today it 'represents' (everything): it is an equivalent, an exchange, a representation: a sign" (*S/Z* 39). Whereas with an index, what represents "is of a different nature from what it indicates," in a sign "the two elements *interchange,* signified and signifier revolving in an endless process: what is bought can be sold, the signified can become signifier, and so on" (40). The exchangeability of signified and signifier associated with a money economy provides further insight into Willy Loman's anxiety regarding the distinguishing of "talk" from "action."

In a world where all value is supplanted by economic value, the consummation of desire is precisely the *end* of value: the "moment of enjoyment itself, when the opposition between subject and object is effaced, consumes the value" (Simmel 66). From the salesman's perspective, this end of value is conveyed in the term "closing the sale." In a sense, Willy never wants to "close" Biff or himself as commodities, for thus ends his hope that their value will rise. At the same time, Willy tries to escape the commodification of identity by his insistence on the existence of a mysterious "greatness" or "personal attractiveness" possessed by Biff and himself, as if the market has priced them incorrectly, has failed to take into account some mysterious, unquantifiable quality. This simultaneous fear of, and clinging to, the market reaches its ultimate end for Willy when he decides that *he* is worth more dead than alive and commits suicide in an attempt to cash in on his insurance policy, effectively turning himself into money.

If Willy has reason to be anxious about money and what it signifies, so too does Biff. From the earliest moments of the play, Biff seems to be viewed by his father primarily in terms of how much money he is earning. The first fight we learn of between Biff and Willy is about money: "I simply asked him if he was making any money," explains Willy, who goes on to complain that after ten years of "tramping around," Biff "has yet to make thirty-five dollars a week" (9). Aside from his father's viewing him as a commodity, Biff is troubled by the existential implications of money, chief among these money's disassociation of appearance from reality, material value from "face" value, or its tendency to treat one as the other (1). This manifests itself in the play as Biff's obsession with the authentic (with a "hard" or natural value) and the opposite, his preference for deceptive appearance over the real. Biff repeatedly accuses Willy of having "no character" or being "a fake" or even (redundantly) a "phoney little fake!" (40, 42, 88). Biff says he wants to find a woman "with substance" (17). Yet when Linda answers his question about her hair suddenly going gray with the explanation that it had been gray for a long time, that she "just stopped dyeing it," Biff seemingly chooses appearance over the real, and asks her to "[d]ye it again" (39). In essence, Biff wants Linda's physical appearance to match his own timeless, unchanging idea of who/what she is.

The contradictions in Biff's attitude toward the real and the symbolic are again embodied in Willy's brother Ben, that representation of money in the play. Ben is Biff's uncle and the family's only link to Willy's father (Biff's grandfather). Willy asks Ben to tell stories about his father so Biff and Happy can "know the kind of stock they spring from" (34). Yet in the one encounter between Ben and Biff that we witness, Ben turns violent during apparent play, tripping Biff and stopping just short of stabbing him in the eye with his umbrella, then admonishing his nephew, "Never fight fair with a stranger, boy. You'll never get out of the jungle that way" (49). The alternately warm and violent Ben, both a family member and a "stranger," here appears in trickster fashion as an uncanny manifestation of Biff's deepest anxieties about money and the gulf it opens between appearance and reality, surface and essence.

Troubled as he is by the existential implications of money, Biff, like other protagonists in this study, enacts a (failed) strategy of "escape" from the money economy – in Biff's case, largely through his propensity to steal. Simmel notes that both in what he calls "primitive" societies as well as among contemporary aristocracy, there is often "a distaste for exchange," with robbery and gift-giving looked at as the more honorable activities (97). The reason for this, the author hypothesizes, is an anxiety concerning the alienation from nature that characterizes economic exchange. Unlike the "objectivity" of economic exchange, theft and gift-giving represent "pure subjectivity in the change of ownership" (97). The stolen or freely given object is not reduced to money, not drained of its individual and irreplaceable qualities. Seen in this light, Biff's frequent stealing (of basketballs [18, 82], a football [20], lumber [36], and finally a pen [76]) represents an attempt to escape the alienating world of economic exchange and thus assuage his anxiety concerning reality and appearances, hard value and soft money.

A second manifestation of Biff's repression of money takes the form of Biff's efforts to escape the technological, commodified city and return to nature. Willy himself in fact repeatedly expresses his own sense of separation from nature: he bemoans the overdevelopment of his Brooklyn neighborhood, complaining to Linda that today, because of the surrounding apartment houses, you "[g]otta break your neck to see a star" in their backyard (350). Willy remembers when "[t]his time of year it was lilac and wisteria," but now buildings stand where once these flowers grew

(340). While the fact that no seeds will grow in that same yard is surely a metaphor for Willy's dashed hopes for his sons, in a larger sense it also comments on Willy's sense of separation from the natural world. By leaving the city and traveling west to work with horses, Biff is in one sense returning to nature. He tells Happy that in Texas "it's spring there now" and conjures images of mares giving birth to new colts (341). Biff's life on the farm represents a return to an experience of time as cyclical, one marked by the passage of seasons, which dictate to a certain degree one's labor (22). Conversely, the city is the place where time is sensed as linear and progressive: it is where you "build a future," where Hap slowly works his way up the corporate ladder, where flowers no longer grow in the back yard, where a man must "add up" to something, not be "ringing up a zero" (125, 126). This marking of the passage of time by natural events (the blooming of lilac, the birthing of the colts) contrasts sharply with a different sense of time, one embodied in Willy's remark that in "ten years" of trying to "find himself," Biff has yet to earn a decent salary (Miller 16). Viewing these two senses of time across many cultures, E.P. Thompson has hypothesized a historical evolution from a pre-industrial sense of "natural" time to a more Protestant sense of time as money, the latter either exacerbated or caused by the Industrial Revolution and the division of labor. Biff's move from country to city is, by this logic, more than just geographical, and represents an attempt to escape the commodification of life implied in Willy's remark about his meager earnings. By associating these two senses of time with the city and the country, the east and the west, Miller's play seems to be partaking in yet another manifestation of the American pastoral, with Texas standing in as the western "green world" where one may escape the pressures of the "civilized" eastern metropolis.[10]

But a closer look reveals something more complicated, for both Willy and Biff are caught between what country and city symbolize in this play in a way that reveals how both are ensnared within a cultural logic associated with money. Texas in fact only seems to offer Biff an escape from the commodified city, for as he explains to Hap, each time he leaves something draws him back to New York:

> Texas is cool now, and it's spring. And whenever spring comes to where I am, I suddenly get the feeling, my God, I'm not gettin' anywhere! What the hell am I doing, playing around with horses, twenty-eight dollars a week! I'm thirty-four years old, I oughta be makin' my future. That's when I come running home. And now, I get here, and I don't know what to do with myself. *(After a pause.)* I've always made a point of not wasting my life, and every time I come back here I know that all I've done is to waste my

life. (341)

What Thompson and Weber identify as the Protestant idea of time as money, as something to be spent or wasted, appears in this passage as a kind of serpent invading Biff's western Eden. Biff exists in a kind of restless stasis. Repeatedly, he attempts to escape the commodified world of the city by moving physically west and working close to the land. But as we've seen, Biff essentially takes the city with him in the form of an internalized set of values that sees the future as something you "build" and the value of a person's life measured in how much he earns. Similarly, upon returning to the world of money symbolically associated with cities and the east, Biff rejects what he sees as a "measly manner of existence" and longs to be back on a western farm.

In *The Country and the City,* Raymond Williams uncovers the way much if not all of our notions of "country" and "city" are the product of capitalist discourse, with its "abstracted economic drives, its fundamental priorities in social relations, its criteria of growth and of profit and loss" (302). This discourse clearly finds voice in Biff's tangled relationship between country and city, where, ironically, the arrival of spring sends Biff running back to the city, and where it is never clear which life – his life on a farm or his life in the city – he considers "wasted." Where the arrival of spring brings Willy to thoughts of lilac and the country, of regeneration through nature, the same season sends Biff back to the city to find another sort of regeneration: an economic one that becomes *more* real to him than nature: to "make" his "future." Similarly, where thoughts of physical labor lead to Willy's anxiety over a perceived lack of seriousness or masculinity in his own profession, Biff now redefines his physical labor on a western farm as "playing around" and associates serious work with the "mental," talk-based labor of sales. Biff's entrapment within these notions of country and city demonstrates the way, in capitalist cultures, the abstract "economy" claims for itself privileged access to the "real," to the "bottom line," transforming at the same time material reality into an abstract idea.

The character of Willy, as we have seen, also complicates distinctions between nature and technology, country and city. Several cultural historians have noted the salesman's unique relation to the technological world. For Earl Shorris, periods of rapid economic expansion tend to position the salesman as "the Prometheus of the machine age," bringing "dozens of basic new ideas to the American public"(68). But in his cultural history of the salesman, Timothy Spears sees the figure's relation to technology as more ambivalent:

> The [nineteenth-century] commercial traveler . . . was the aggressive, logical consequence of the expanding national market system, a figure who from an economic standpoint remained inseparable from the growth of the railroad and other developments that strengthened the 'visible hand' of business . . . . Yet . . . the traveling salesman's relation to these forces did not wholly determine the development of his sales techniques nor make him the pawn of institutional forces. In fact, it often provided him with a modicum of freedom, although not without some cost" ("Preface" xi).

In one sense, the salesman is both a commodity and a piece of technology; in another sense, the salesman (especially the traveling salesman) escapes, to a degree, the confining, "rationalized" workplace he helps to create. The salesman working for commission is freer, in a sense, than the salaried worker; at the same time, he makes of himself that purely instrumental thing: a commodity. From the individual buyer's viewpoint, the salesman is both the tool of the market and the one human element in what otherwise faces the consumer as a vast, depersonalized marketplace. From the salesman's viewpoint, technology – in the form of the mass-produced goods he sells and the technologies of transportation (trains, automobiles, hotel rooms) and communication that make his job possible – is a paradox he lives with daily. As a human being in an increasingly streamlined marketplace, the salesman fears being replaced by technology, and strives to "modernize" his profession, to turn selling into a science, himself into a kind of selling machine. As a piece of technology himself, he fears being replaced by new technology, which is of course the fate of all technology by its very nature. The "Prometheus of the machine age" is both humanized technology and technologized humanity, a portent of the future and a superannuated relic of the past. He is at once too human and too much a piece of technology. Of the traveling salesman of the first quarter of the twentieth century, Spears writes:

> Despite the claims to modernity that ran throughout the literature, the salesman remained only human, which is to say that no matter how scientific his rhetoric or approach appeared, he represented the continuity of face-to-face relationships in a world increasingly given to effacing them. Janus-faced, the twentieth-century traveling man was neither drummer nor scientific salesman, but frequently and sometimes tragically he was both. (7)

Brenda Murphy looks at reactions in the business press to Willy Loman from the time of the play's first production to the present, and finds a similarly paradoxical relationship between the salesman and technology: "If only he had had better sales training, or better job counseling, or a laptop computer," the business press contends, Willy would be a success.

Thus, the "anxiety of having to master new technology, or at worst, of being replaced by it, is displaced by a hopeful rhetoric that suggests technology might be the salesman's salvation" *(Willy Loman: Icon of Business Culture* 762).

Miller has written that Willy Loman is "seeking for a kind of ecstasy in life, which the machine-civilization deprives people of" (qtd. In Bloom 45). But a close reading of *Salesman* reveals a more ambivalent attitude toward technology than Miller's comment suggests. Here, Heidegger's analysis of technology is useful: technology not simply as the use of tools or the application of machinery, but as a deeply-rooted mindset, a way of being that places the human subject in a certain relation to his surroundings, to other people, and to himself. It is characterized by a view of everything and everyone as available to be manipulated: what was once thought of as the earth "now reveals itself as a coal mining district, the soil as a mineral deposit [. . .] Agriculture is now the mechanized food industry. Air is now set upon to yield nitrogen, the earth to yield ore, ore to yield uranium" (Heidegger 324, 320). Everything, including human beings (which technology transforms into "human resources") is thought of as "immediately on hand" to be used, as "standing-reserve *[Bestand]"* (322). Using the example of a hydroelectric plant set into the Rhine, Heidegger illustrates the way technology decides being, and, as in Marx's treatment of money, Heidegger invokes the trope of monstrosity:

> What the river is now, namely, a water-power supplier, derives from the essence of the power station. In order that we may even remotely consider the monstrousness that reigns here, let us ponder for a moment the contrast that is spoken by the two titles: "The Rhine," as dammed up into the *power* works, and "The Rhine," as uttered by the *art*-work, in Hölderlein's hymn by that name. But, it will be replied, the Rhine is still a river in the landscape, is it not? Perhaps. But how? In no other way than as an object on call for inspection by a tour group ordered there by the vacation industry. (321)

Technology conceived in this way constitutes a kind of paradox. The world as standing reserve "no longer stands over against us as object," and so becomes less threatening, less alien, precisely because it is serviceable to our needs (322). At the same time, we cannot "step outside" technology. Heidegger expresses this complex situation this way:

> As soon as what is unconcealed no longer concerns man even as object, but exclusively as standing-reserve, . . . then he comes to the very brink of a precipitous fall; that is, he comes to the point where he himself will have to be taken as standing-reserve. Meanwhile, man, precisely as the one so

> threatened, exalts himself and postures as lord of the earth. In this way the illusion comes to prevail that everything man encounters exists only insofar as it is his construct. This illusion gives rise in turn to one final delusion: it seems as though man everywhere and always encounters only himself . . . . *In truth, however, precisely nowhere does man today any longer encounter himself, i.e., his essence.* (332)

This tangled relationship to technology is represented with particular force early in the second act of the play, when Willy goes to see his boss, Howard Wagner, in an attempt to gain a salaried position in New York. Here, Willy tries to establish a personal connection with Howard by bringing up the warm relationship he once had with Howard's father – to establish a relationship on a more "essential" ground than as an employee talking to his boss. Initially, Howard is too preoccupied with a new piece of technology to even notice Willy. Howard describes the new wire-recording machine in a way that belies his own paradoxical relation to technology: this "most terrific machine [he] ever saw" has kept him "up all night" and is "driving [him] crazy" (76). Offering a more "fascinating relaxation," the recorder will, he tells Willy, replace his camera, his bandsaw, and "all [his] hobbies" (78). An office machine that has also become a family toy, the wire-recorder embodies the role of technology in breaking down boundaries between work and home. Willy is forced to listen to Howard's son recite the state capitals. Howard's wife, whom the stage directions characterize as *"beaten,"* is forced by Howard the manager/husband to speak into the machine, as a piece of technology becomes that which *compels* speech: "Well, talk," commands Howard, "it's turning." His son announces mechanically that it is "nine o'clock, Bulova watch time" and thus time to go to bed, illustrating E.P. Thompson's thesis of the replacement of "natural" time with clock time in a way that also emphasizes the ominous role of corporate power in this process (it is *Bulova* watch time). At the same time, Howard points out that by using the recorder to tape his favorite radio shows, he gains a kind of control over time: "You can come home twelve o'clock, one o'clock, any time you like, and you get yourself a Coke and sit yourself down, throw the switch, and there's Jack Benny's program in the middle of the night!" (78). The mention of specific products – Coke and Jack Benny's program – emphasizes the dubious nature of the freedom offered by Howard's newest piece of technology, presenting Howard as "standing-reserve" for both the soft drink companies as well as the entertainment industry that exists largely for the purpose of selling its products through advertising. But the more Howard appears as standing-reserve, the more does he convince himself that he can reconfigure the world to suit his desires, with technology at the very nexus of this contradiction.

Salesman ultimately complicates, rather than reinforces, the distinction between country and city, technology and nature. If the play alerts us to a problem, that problem cannot be isolated as a specifically urban or technological one; rather, the capitalistic economic values the play investigates appear in both country and city – where do they seem more prevalent than in Ben's "jungle"? – and in fact reconfigure our very notions of country and city. New York City is where you "build a future," yet Willy spends all his work time in the "New England Territory," itself a term that calls to mind the conflicting images of an open frontier and industrial cities like Boston, Hartford, and Providence.

By the end of the play, Willy and Biff have the confrontation that has been building through the entire action of the play – but their argument resembles two men attempting to escape from the same net rather than the clash of two fundamentally different ideas. Biff would reject Willy's money-centered mentality, even as he calls himself "one dollar an hour" and argues that he and his father are both "a dime a dozen," thus demonstrating his own inability to think of himself as other than commodity (132). Willy argues for an identity not lashed to the marketplace – "I am not a dime a dozen! I am Willy Loman and you are Biff Loman!" (132) – and then kills himself in an attempt to turn himself into cash in Biff's pocket. In the "Requiem" that closes the play, Happy only condemns Willy's suicide on the grounds that "[t]here was no necessity for it," as if his suicide would be fine if it proved economically *useful* (137). And Charley – the man who once chillingly invited Willy to think of Biff as a broken bottle that will not return its nickel deposit (31) – rewrites the tragedy of Willy as a paean to the salesman: "A salesman is got to dream, boy; it comes with the territory" (101). In ironic contrast to Linda's repeated "We're free" at Willy's graveside, the characters of Miller's play are as trapped as they ever were.

In his legendary 1936 advice book, *How to Win Friends and Influence People,* Dale Carnegie advises the successful persuader to "[b]ecome genuinely interested in other people" and to "[m]ake the other person feel important --and do it sincerely" (111). This *use* of one's personality illustrates how, in C. Wright Mills' words, the marketplace in the twentieth century "has at once become more impersonal and more intimate" (161). A "self-alienation" is felt by more and more people as "the cash nexus that links one man to another in transient contact has been made subtle in a dozen ways and made to bite deeper into all areas of life and relations." "People are required," writes Mills, "by the salesman ethic and convention to pretend interest in others in order to manipulate them"

(188).

Perhaps the salesman represents something more complicated than a mere "pretending." In his 1990 sociological study of the insurance salesman, Guy Oakes finds what he labels a "Paradox of Sincerity" at the heart of sales. The agents he studies seem to him incredibly sincere about their interest in their customers and their belief in their own honesty and moral soundness. Yet "the sincerity of agents about their trustworthiness creates a paradox," since it "depends upon behavior that casts this very sincerity in doubt: the management of impressions undertaken to convince the prospect to believe in the agent's trustworthiness" (78). As Oakes's comments make clear, the salesman complicates easy distinctions between sincerity and pretending, appearance and reality, performance and authenticity. A profoundly destabilizing figure, Martin Dworkin describes the salesman as "not quite the friend and not quite the enemy and not quite the instrument of the people to whom he is selling" (*"Death of a Salesman:* A Symposium" 44). It is this state of eluding categorization and thus of revealing something even as it conceals it for which Heidegger coined the term *"unheimlich,"* commonly translated into English as "uncanny*."* Developing the term for his own use, Freud defines it as "on the one hand, [. . .] that which is familiar and congenial, and on the other, that which is concealed and kept out of sight" (129). It is also "that class of the terrifying which leads back to something long known to us, once very familiar" (123-4). As that which is at once known and unknown, the uncanny is, according to Freud, a kind of "testing" of reality (156). That which presents itself as uncanny is familiar enough to beg classification, yet utterly eludes such classification, and thus leads to more profound doubts about the picture of the world one has formed for oneself. Freud's example of choice is the automaton, which by its very nature leads us to question the ontological categories of the organic and the mechanical. For the very same reasons, the salesman is in a profound sense a manifestation of the uncanny. In a time when all values are rapidly being replaced by use values; when a ubiquitous marketplace that, as Simmel says, "hangs together like nature" essentially *becomes* the world we all live in, the salesman, by problematizing distinctions such as mechanical and organic, future and past, talk and action, face value and material value, is himself a kind of "testing" of this reality. He is at once a powerful example of reification – of the transformation of the materially real into the abstract and the abstract into the materially real (into the "bottom line," or "hard-headed" economic reality) – and, for this very reason, a monstrous figure that demands that we imagine a different way of being, a way of conceiving human relationships that is not primarily economic.

Moreover, this "testing" of reality is something the salesman shares with Miller's medium of choice: theatre. Interestingly, Oakes compares the salesman's situation to that of the dramatic actor. "To manage impressions," writes Oakes, "is to create a performance, to produce a show." The salesman's work, like the actor's, requires "a distinction between the agent and the character he or she represents." Salesmen, like theatrical performers, must "see themselves both as performers and as the characters that are the product of the performance . . . The logic of the dramaturgic situation guarantees that agents self-consciously represent themselves as what they are not" (78-79). Both money and the commodified persona of the salesman complicate distinctions between hard, "natural" value and representation. In many ways the natural medium for exploring this aspect of both money and the salesman is theatre – itself, when it is at its most powerful, an uncanny "testing" of reality, where simple distinctions between material and face value, reality and appearance, are complicated. In the American theatre, a comparably powerful dissection of the salesman – and of the commodification of life – would not appear until David Mamet's 1984 masterpiece *Glengarry Glenn Ross*. While that work is haunted by Miller's play and revisits many of *Salesman's* themes (especially the tangled distinction between "talk" and action), it is an earlier play of Mamet's that more profoundly investigates the symbolic importance of money.

CHAPTER FOUR

"REAL CLASSICAL MONEY": THE DUBIOUS REDEMPTION OF ECONOMIC LIFE IN DAVID MAMET'S *AMERICAN BUFFALO*

In an essay entitled "Black as the Ace of Spades," David Mamet notes that a group of men may be handed a deck of cards, but will not engage in poker if no money is involved. Once money is involved, those men will play "for hours or for days." At the same time, "even the reward of money to be won is not enough inducement to those men to push that money back and forth for hours unless they also happen to be holding cards." Mamet concludes, "it's not just the money, and it's not just the cards. But you put the two together and a magic is created." The word "magic" is not used lightly here. Mamet continues:

> The game is not about money. The game is about love, and divine intervention. The money is a propitiatory gift to the Gods. It is the equivalent of Fasting and Prayer: it is to gain the God's attention, and to put the supplicant in the properly humbled frame of mind to receive any information which might be forthcoming. (*Some Freaks* 172-3)

In thinking performatively about one of his favorite pastimes, treating the poker game as both theatre and ritual, Mamet transfigures money into prop and ritual object, only one among others (such as the playing cards). The game will not proceed without the money, but neither will the money change hands without the cards. The money itself is, in fact, not even money: it is a "gift" to the gods, a kind of sacrifice. Whereas Simmel traced money's "evolution" from means to the ultimate end, Mamet's description would redeem poker by transforming money from end back into means, and reimagining the players not as greedy (or seedy) chasers after greenbacks, but supplicants in a ceremony seeking "divine intervention." Perhaps most surprisingly, this intensely competitive game that necessitates lying (or bluffing) is ultimately about "love."

In *American Buffalo,* the first of Mamet's three "business" plays, which would be followed in 1984 by *Glengarry Glen Ross* and in 1988 by

Speed-the-Plow, the playwright strives to do for American business (and for economic life generally) what the passage quoted here does for poker. In this play about the planning of a never-to-be-committed robbery by junkshop owner Don Dubrow, his "friend and associate" Walter "Teach" Cole, and his young "gopher" Bob, Mamet complicates the naturalist distinction between talk and action, soft currency and hard value, exploring the dislocating effects of both money and language, and ultimately striving to find a place for both in loving relations between men.

In the beginning of the first act, Mamet reveals the philosophical dilemmas raised by money as the primary concern of *American Buffalo* through his protagonist Don Dubrow, whose lessons on business imparted to the young gopher Bob nicely foreground issues central to the logic of naturalism. The first of these conflicts involves what is for many critics the defining theme of literary naturalism: the conflict between one's sense of free will and one's sense of behavior as determined. In discussing Fletcher – the winner of the card game that precedes the action of the play, and one of Mamet's many Godot-like characters representing powerful off-stage forces – Don evokes the paradox of human freedom through his own paradoxical use of the terms "skill," "talent," and "experience." First Don ascribes Fletcher's prowess at cards to "[s]kill and talent and the balls to arrive at your own *conclusions,"* which implies some mixture of a priori ability, learned experience, and independent thinking (4). But then Don asks Bob rhetorically of Fletcher, "was he born that way or do you think he had to learn it?" When Bob dutifully responds "Learn it," Don rewards him with a "Goddamn right he did," and further entrenches himself on the side of experience by claiming that "[e]verything that I or Fletcher know we picked up on the street" (6). Then just when it appears Don is firmly on the side of free will and the ability to learn from experience, he muddles the issue again with the first of this play's several definitions of "business": "That's all business is [. . .] common sense, experience, and talent" (6). Here the two poles of experience (which is learned) and talent (which is innate) are combined with common sense – that dubious mantra of business rhetoric that somehow denotes something both innate *and* learned.

On one level of course Mamet is commenting on the irrational invocation of both unfettered free will and a hard determinism that has always informed the rhetoric of business, and specifically of sales – a theme the playwright would flesh out in his next "business" play, *Glengarry Glen Ross.* In that play, real estate salesmen invoke "skill" to explain their occasional victories but blame their usual failures on a menu of determining factors: bad leads, a poor economy, bad luck. In the 1992 film based on the play, the philosophical paradox – and naturalist obsession – behind the salesmen's griping is emphasized through a message on a chalkboard hanging in the real estate office proclaiming "Salesmen are born not made." The presence of this message turns the salesmen's petty self-doubt into existential horror reminiscent of Willy Loman's search for internal "greatness" in the face of his, and his son Biff's, own failure in the marketplace. As in Miller's play, Mamet's work inscribes the salesman as the embodiment of that naturalist preoccupation with the conflict between "beast and soul" that has been an obsession of modern drama at least since Ibsen. In *American Buffalo* this obsession informs Don's discussion of luck, skill, and talent.

Closely related to this theme, and also an obsession of both the boardroom and the stage, is the naturalist conflict between material reality and representation that pervades *American Buffalo* – and Mamet's entire opus – in the form of a preoccupation with the distinction, or the lack of one, between "talk" and "action." This talk/action distinction, previously explored by Miller, is a subject of Mamet's work much commented on by critics.[11] Thomas King notes that another of Don's business lessons for Bob, that "[a]ction talks and bullshit walks," is another way of saying in fact that action talks and talk acts – in other words, that action *is* talk and talk *is* action. This seeming paradox is a central truth in the work of both the playwright and the salesman, both of whose "action" takes the form of words. "Conflict may be the heart of dramatic action," notes King, "but the heart of conflict is talk" (539). That Don is both aware of and troubled by this paradox is clear in the way he tries repeatedly to control the "talk" of other characters in the play. When Teach, in an attempt to replace Bob as Don's accomplice in the planned robbery, subtly refers to Bob's heroin addiction, Don interjects, "I don't want you mentioning that," and a few lines later, "I don't want that talk" (34). In the second act there are two more instances of Don's trying to limit the "talk" of Teach. When Teach, now trying to eliminate Fletcher from the robbery, tells Don he's "full of shit," Don responds "Don't tell me that" and "I don't want that talk" (74). Again, when Teach tells Don near the end of the play that Fletcher cheats at cards, Don responds, "You're *telling* me this? . . . I don't want to hear it" (80). Don rightly fears the "talk" of Teach. These instances of Don's trying to limit what other characters *say* demonstrate Don's understanding of talk as action, as that which creates reality rather than merely representing or referring to a reality "outside" that talk. In spite of the hard distinction he would like to draw between talk and action, Don seems to possess a more complicated understanding of the relation of word to deed.

If Don's fear of certain kinds of "talk" can be explained by his being, after all, a salesman and a businessman – one who understands talk *as action* – more difficult to explain is Don's relation to that which constitutes the very essence of his profession: the acts of buying and selling. It is worth mentioning that nowhere in the play do we see this salesman *sell* anything. In fact, the one item we are *told* of his selling – the buffalo nickel whose sale precedes the action of the play – Don spends the entire play trying to get back. The motive for this planned robbery is not pecuniary, as Christopher Bigsby has pointed out (72). A perceived loss of honor, rather than any desire for money, is what motivates Don. In fact, when Teach brings up the issue of the relative value of the different coins the two imagine to be in their would-be victim's possession, Don is not interested, and insists "First off, I want that nickel back" – that though "it's only a fuckin' nickel" he wants it back and does not seem to care what the man's other coins may be worth (45).

Unsurprisingly, Don's seemingly strange aversion to buying and selling are reflected in his language. In the first act, Don's refusal to use the words "buy" or "sell" – in situations that seem clearly to call for those words – is difficult to ignore. He sends Bob to "get" (not "buy") some coffee and yogurt. When Bob answers Don's suggestion that he take vitamins with the hard economic fact that he "can't afford" vitamins, which are "expensive," Don says oddly, "Don't worry about it. You should just take em," as if money were no object. In case we still fail to pick up on Don's aversion to (or repression of) buying, Mamet has Bob ask for clarification: "You'll buy some for me?" Don replies, "I'll get you some" (9). Similarly, when Don later pays Bob for spotting the coin collector, he speaks of it not as a payment but as a gift: "I'm *giving* you twenty-five" (43). Even in his telling of the transaction between himself and the coin buyer, Don seems unwilling or unable to speak of buying or selling. The buyer "*takes*" the nickel, he "takes me off my coin" (31). When Don does once use a form of the verb "to buy," he does so in a paradoxical way: the man, he says, "bought the buffalo off me," the use of "off" rather than the more conventional "from" implying a number of things: a personal relationship between Don and his merchandise (though Don admits he did not even know the nickel was in his case prior to the buyer's discovering it), a view of the purchase as a kind of theft, and even a view of the purchase as the lifting of a burden from Don. Don, apparently, can only bring himself to speak of exchange as gift or theft, not as purchase.

As a salesman, and more specifically a "junkshop" owner, who seems to demonstrate a bizarre aversion to selling anything in his possession, Don resembles a character from a work synonymous with literary naturalism: Norris's *McTeague.* Benn Michaels notes that in that novel, the junkshop owner Zerkow is described as "a man who accumulates, but never disburses" merchandise, making his shop in effect "the last abiding-place, the almshouse, of such articles as had outlived their usefulness" (qtd. in Michaels 153). Don Dubrow similarly seems to accumulate but never disburse his "junk." As a salesman with an aversion to buying and selling, Don, like Zerkow, emerges as a powerful embodiment of the naturalist repression of money.

Is there a relation between Don's sensitivity to "talk" and his repression of money (or at least of buying and selling)? A clue may lie in a strange thing Don says about rare coins. When Bob, who in the second act is trying to sell a different buffalo nickel to Don, suggests that some discontinued coins are worth a lot of money, Don answers that such coins are "[f]reak oddities of nature" (61). The odd implication of this statement, of course, is that money is somehow *natural.* The idea – the fantasy – of "natural" money is perhaps the most important feature of the logic of naturalism. In the arguments put forth by the goldbugs and the silver men during the gold standard controversy in America, for all their political differences, the two camps shared a tendency to see precious metals as "nature embodied" (Benn Michaels 147). In their rejection of "greenbacks" or paper money, both the gold and the silver men rejected what they saw as an "unnatural" and therefore inadequate currency in favor of one with *intrinsic* value. Unlike paper money, which stood for a value located elsewhere, the "natural" money of the precious metal was seen as containing in itself the value it signified – the metal, unlike paper money, *is* what it *represents.* Of course, such "natural" money is in fact no money at all, for in a "natural" economy wherein the units of money were also the value they referred to, all money exchanges would also be barter exchanges. "The assertion that money exists in nature," Benn Michaels notes, "is thus identical to the assertion that money doesn't exist at all" (148). Thus were both the goldbug and the silver man engaged in "a failed attempt to withdraw from the money economy, failed because in a money economy, the power of money to buy can never be denied" (140). The existence of a money economy, like the existence of language, requires an acceptance of signification – an agreement that one thing may stand for another. The repression of money, the attempt to "escape" the money economy, is the expression of an anxiety concerning the unavoidable tendency of signifiers to mislead. By implying that money is "natural," Mamet's tragic hero expresses a wish that money and the existential uncertainty it signifies did not exist – that, despite the advice he gives Bob to the contrary, things *are* what they *seem.*

Or is Don's wish that, as his antagonist Walter "Teach" Cole says to Bob in the first act, "[t]hings are what they are" (39)? Teach makes his enigmatic comment during an attempt to convince Don that he (Teach), not Bobby, is the right man to pull off the robbery. He accomplishes this con through a strange demonstration of Bob's supposed ignorance, which begins with Teach's asking Bob a deceptively innocent question about the weather: does Bob think it will rain? When Bob's answer, understandably, expresses some uncertainty, Teach implies that this somehow shows Bob's ignorance (38). This is because the weather forecast, like so many things for Teach, is self-evident. When Don asks Teach earlier in the first act if he thinks it will rain, Teach responds absurdly, "Yeah. I do. Later" (20). When Don questions Teach's certainty on this point Teach replies, "Well, *look* at it" (20). The weather, for Teach, is self-evident, unmediated presence; if Bob does not know if it will rain he simply is not seeing what is right in front of his nose.

The next part of Teach's con to discredit Bob in Don's eyes takes the form of a question about an object in Don's shop, which Don has only just explained to Teach is a device used for draining the blood from a dead pig. When Bob obviously does not know what the device is (despite his protests that he *does* know what it is – he is beginning to catch on to Teach's game), Teach imparts the wisdom that things "are what they are." At first glance this seems like a refutation of the advice Don gives Bob earlier in the first act: "Things are not always what they seem" (8). But Teach is not saying that things are what they *seem*; he is saying that they are what they *are.* In this formulation, "seeming" itself is denied, in keeping with what unfolds in the course of the play as Teach's total denial of signification. For Teach, as we will see, there is the real and there is language or "talk,' and the two rarely if ever have anything to do with one another.

To place Teach's philosophy in proper context, it is important to note that in other Mamet plays and screenplays, the most deceptive character is the one who espouses just this view of perception as an uncomplicated, totally transparent act. In Mamet's 1987 film *House of Games,* the con-man Mike (Joe Mantegna) tantalizes the psychiatrist Margaret Ford (Lindsay Crouse) with the notion of the "tell": a physical tic that supposedly reveals when a card player is bluffing (15). Similarly, in Mamet's 1994 play *The Cryptogram,* the character Del, who we will learn has deceived the other two characters, declares early in the first act that " a human *being* [. . .] cannot conceal himself." When the child John asks for more explanation, Del begins, in true Teach fashion, "Well, hell, *look* at it" (5). Likewise in the screenplay for Mamet's 1997 Hitchcockian thriller, *The*

Spanish Prisoner, a character perhaps not coincidentally named Julian "Jimmy" Dell (played by Steve Martin) espouses a similar faith in the self-evident nature of observable reality: "People aren't that complicated, Joe. Good people, bad people . . . they generally look like what they are" (46). Of course, Del, Mike, and Julian Dell all turn out to be dangerous and amoral masters of deception. As in these other works, *American Buffalo* invites us to criticize the stated position of Teach that things "are what they are" as a kind of confidence game perpetrated, in this case, on Don, a character deeply suspicious of appearances and desperate for solid foundations.

Teach's statement that things "are what they are" also marks an important distinction between himself and Don. Whereas Don is troubled by the ambiguities involved in signification – whether that signification is in the form of "talk" or money – Teach seems to view all signs as completely divorced from "reality." Repeatedly in this play, Teach asserts his apparent belief in the complete impossibility of any utterance's corresponding with the "truth." When Don, in the first act, tries to calm Teach down by telling him it is "all right" that Bob spoke to Ruth about Teach's anger toward her despite Teach's asking him not to, Teach responds, "Everything's all right to *someone*" (21). Just a few lines later, Teach, who seems to exist on a diet of bacon and coffee, tries to convince Don that yogurt (Don's favorite food) is bad for one's health. When Don disagrees, Teach again falls back on his own theory of relativity: "Each one his own opinion" – as if the health value of a particular food were *wholly* a matter of opinion, impossible to be decided on any kind of factual basis (21).

Teach thus seems to espouse the following two positions: first, that we have easy access to an essential, self-evident reality (just *look* at it); and second, that language is a system of endless signification with no meaningful relation to that reality. As the embodiment of these two seemingly inconsistent positions, Teach is the perfect antagonist for Don. Teach's language games and endless subterfuges confirm Don's worst fear: the lack of an essential, "hard" reality, a lack he associates with both money and language. At the same time, Teach's insistence on a clear, self-evident, extra-lingual, and essential reality tantalizes Don, for, as Teach seems to sense, this is precisely what Don most wants to believe. In the manner of Mamet's other confidence men, Teach attempts to both seduce and confuse Don with the message that all is what it is, transcendentally and extra-lingually knowable, and that nothing is what it *seems.* When Don disagrees with Teach's assertion that he (Don) treats Bob as more than a business associate, Teach states "In your mind you don't, but the things, I'm saying, that you actually go *do* for him. This is fantastic" (34). According to Teach, Don's subjective view of his own relationship with Bobby is one thing, the reality of that relationship another thing entirely. Near the end of the second act, when Don tells Teach he does not like Teach's showing up late, Teach responds, "Then *don't* like it, then. Let's do this. Let's everybody get a writ. I got a case. You got a case" (64). For Teach, apparently, everyone has his or her own, and equally valid (or invalid) interpretation of the "facts." A truthful single perspective on the real cannot exist. In excusing his own lateness, Teach even casts doubt on our ability to ever know what time it is: "And so who knows precisely what time it is offhand? Jerks on the radio? The phone broad?" (64).

In the absence of a "hard" truth, Teach attempts to coerce Don and Bob into making decisions that benefit Teach, and he does this through language. It is important to note that both Don and Teach recognize the ambiguity and misdirection inherent in language. But whereas Don fears this ambiguity as an obstacle to the truth, Teach welcomes it as a means to attain power. Ultimately it does not seem to matter to Teach that language is divorced from the real, for Teach's goal is not to know but to manipulate. If Don is sensitive to what language can *do,* the speech-acts that concern him are those that could poison his paternal relationship to Bob or smear the reputation of Fletcher, a man for whom he has great respect (both of these things Teach's "talk" threatens to do, and Don attempts to prevent both by limiting that talk). Teach, conversely, is concerned only about speech-acts that either extend or limit his power. In this and other respects, Teach is not unlike the character of Ben in Miller's *Death of a Salesman.* Ben professes a fondness for "hard" reality, for things you can "lay your hand on" (Miller 360). Teach relentlessly appeals to "facts," to "the way *things* are"(Mamet 85). Ben is impatient with Willy's penchant for "talk." Teach similarly devalues talk. "I can sit here and tell you *this,* I can tell you *that,* I can tell you any fucking thing you care to mention," he tells Don near the end of the play, "but what is the point" (79)? Both characters, moreover, represent a kind of moral relativism. Ben famously advises Biff to "never fight fair with a stranger," as he advocates the ethics, or lack of them, that got him "out of the jungle" (Miller 49). According to Teach, "you make your own right and wrong" (Mamet 52).

The glaring, often funny, and definitely sinister contradiction embodied by Teach is that while he convinces (for a time) the other characters of the play that they are essentially trapped inside their own consciousness, he claims for himself a kind of magical ability to gain direct access to objective "reality." Twice in the play Teach alarms Don and Bob by claiming to see a police car riding slowly by the store. The other characters simply take his word for this car's existence, and he lets them know when the car has passed (29, 85). This nicely symbolizes the implicit message of Teach's con game: all *you* can know is your own subjective reality; I, on the other hand, deal in "facts." Trust me, and I'll let you know what's really going on "out there." "A fact," Teach tells Don, "stands by itself. And we must face the facts and act on them" (75). A few lines later Teach announces, "I am a businessman, I am here to do business, I am here to face facts" (83). But only Teach, apparently, has access to these facts: "You live in a world of your own, Don" (80). When Teach shows up in the last act with a gun, and Don says "I don't like it," Teach responds, "Don't look at it," as if we could all create the reality we like by only allowing those things into our consciousness of which we approve. But then Teach says he needs the gun because of "[t]he light of things as they are," and again, "[b]ecause of the way *things* are" (85). This argument is of course interrupted by the second of Teach's supposed sightings of police cruisers outside the store. We are all trapped inside a system of endless signification in which meaning is always deferred, implies Teach; oh and by the way, I know what's *really* going on.

By thus divorcing material from representation, Teach becomes the uncanny embodiment of a major component of the logic of naturalism, one implicated in the anxiety associated with money. Teach thus appears as an avatar of this awareness of the tenuous and arbitrary relationship between material and representation that has accompanied the increasing symbolization of money. Like Ben in *Death of a Salesman* and Baby-Face Martin in Kingsley's *Dead End,* Teach is the uncanny embodiment of money and its tendency to problematize "hard" distinctions between appearance and reality. More disturbingly, Teach also represents what Marx recognized as money's power to turn economic abstractions into the "real" and human realities into abstractions. The "facts" that he claims he is here to "face" are of course phantoms created by him, and the real human needs of Don and Bob become abstract figments of Don's imagination.

In order to make sense of how the agon between Don and Teach plays out, we need first to return briefly to Don's attempts to escape the money economy whose paradoxes Teach embodies. In addition to Don's fear of "talk," his repression of money, and his attempt to view money as "natural," there are two more factors worth considering: the planning of the robbery itself, and that titular nickel.

Much of the complexity of the play is borne of the fact that what appear to be Don's "lower" motives are in another sense his higher motives. The play opens with Don's advice to Bob concerning the ethics of business, the gist of which is to keep things impersonal. While Don tells Bob that "there's business and there's friendship," essentially his advice is to treat *all* relationships like business relationships. Don demonstrates this attitude in his manner toward Bob. When the latter offers an apology for failing to keep track of the coin buyer's movements, Don says, "Don't tell me you're sorry. I'm not mad at you" (4). Again, when Bob thanks Don for offering to "get" him some vitamins, Don's response reflects a cold focus on utility rather than anything like friendship: "Don't thank *me* . . . I just can't use you in here like a zombie." When Bob then offers yet another explanation for his failure, Don responds, "I don't care. Do you see? Do you see what I'm getting at" (9)? What Don is "getting at" seems to be that in business, all relationships should be governed by a coolly detached self-interest. The reader is invited to see this philosophy as immoral, as the corrupting of personal relationships by the "business values" to which Teach claims allegiance; consider, however, that the planning of the robbery, which in one sense is the beginning of Don's fall, is at the same time Don's rejection of the alienating, impersonal world of the money economy. The man's buying the nickel was "just business," as Teach tries to remind Don, but Don takes it personally. The cool detachment that Don seems unable to attain here is a necessary part of economic life, wherein individuals must be able to calmly bid on what they desire in place of simply taking it. Robbery, conversely, is characterized by "pure subjectivity in the change of ownership," as is the giving of gifts" (Simmel 98). In this sense, Don's desire to get his nickel back through robbery, clearly motivated by a sense of injured honor rather than a desire for money, constitutes in an interesting way a rejection of the alienating world of economic exchange. The planned robbery itself, then, represents yet another attempt at escaping the money economy, and it does so in a way that implicates the audience in the depersonalized world of economic relations. Most of us see the planned robbery as morally repugnant, and probably view Don's angry reaction to a legitimate sale as absurd. But in reacting this way, we endorse Don's cold business advice to Bob not to take anything "personal." It is the sinister Teach, after all, who reminds Don that his personal feelings toward their intended victim do not matter: "The guy's an asshole or he's not, what do you care? It's business" (28).

Finally, Don Dubrow's failed attempt to stage the disappearance of money is symbolized by the titular nickel that incites the talk/action of *American Buffalo.* As a unit of currency that transforms into a work of art (and Don refers to it as "real Classical money"[36]), the buffalo nickel is a powerful symbol of both the desire for, and the impossibility of, escape from the money economy. Once valued, like all circulating currency, not for what it materially "is" but for the value it represents, the now-discontinued buffalo nickel becomes a collector's item and so re-enters the realm of material "things": whereas one normal, circulating nickel is as good as another – its individual, material reality does not matter – each Buffalo nickel is one of a kind, its value varying widely according to its date, condition, and a number of other factors. But while in this sense the nickel seems to escape the money economy, it also simultaneously re-enters that economy as a commodity whose value can be fixed, to a certain degree, and listed in the "blue book" Don shows to Teach in the second act. This doomed attempt to escape the money economy is not particular to rare coins, of course. Any antique object, and any work of art, that becomes desired not for what it either does or represents but for what it materially *is* embodies this same fantasy of escape, with the same predictable results: the object is lifted high above the base marketplace by nature of its being deemed a "classic"; then of course it is priced accordingly. Today, popular TV programs like "The Antiques Road Show" reenact this process ten times in an hour for the enjoyment of millions of viewers who, perhaps, obtain a comforting sense of control by witnessing a repeated re-enactment of the origins of the money economy – a kind of Freudian *fort-da* game in which commodities seem to escape, then re-enter, the money economy repeatedly.[12]

In fact, the antique embodies this process even more powerfully than the "pure' work of art, because the antique is a *useful* object that is now valued not for its usefulness but for some other quality that is harder to pin down – its "presence" or what Benjamin calls its "aura." Finally, antique money even more powerfully embodies the need for, and the impossibility of, escape from the money economy and the signification it embodies, since money is that most useful, most instrumental of objects. Thus the transformation of money into art (into "real Classical money") represents the most desperate and most doomed search for origins and essences "outside" or "underneath" the marketplace.

In *American Buffalo,* Don's denial of that same, anxiety-generating money economy helps explain his refusal to recognize the actual price of either the buffalo nickel he sold or the one Bob brings him at the end of Act II. Once he sells the first nickel for ninety dollars, Don speculates that it must be worth more than that, though he admits he does not know for sure. But in the second act we learn that Don has a "blue book" of coin prices, though he does not seem particularly anxious to consult it. When Teach suggests they use the book to learn the prices of various coins their mark may have in his possession, Don claims "All the values aren't *current*" and that the book only "gives you a general idea" (47, 48). The anxiety Don attaches to fixing the price – even within a "general idea" – of the buffalo nickel is evident again in his negotiations with Bob over a second buffalo nickel in Act II. When Bob suggests that they can refer to the book to ascertain the price of the coin, Don demurs: "Well, no. What I'm saying, the book is like an *indicator*" (61).

This last comment about the blue book occurs during the second act, when Bob returns ostensibly to offer Don a second buffalo nickel that he says he "found" (59). Left deeply suspicious by the verbal manipulations of Teach in the first act, Don tries to get at the *real* reason Bob has returned to the shop. What Don does not see is that the coin Bob claims to want to sell to Don is, for Bob, merely a pretense – a prop, if you will – for what he's really after: the reestablishment of a bond of affection between himself and Don that he rightly perceives has been broken by the manipulative Teach. It is "talk" of the sort Teach despises that Bob is after – "talk" in the sense of conversation whose real subject is the establishment of warm relations between the speakers, not the ostensible subject of the negotiation encoded in that speech. The now deeply distrustful Don cannot see this, and ascribes a manipulative motive to everything Bob says. When the latter mentions that he saw Grace and Ruthie (the offstage female characters with whom Teach is feuding throughout the play) at the diner, Don goes on the attack: "What the fuck does that mean?" (60). Bobby responds, "I didn't *mean* anything" (60). Then Don and Bob enter into a rather strange sort of negotiation. Don repeatedly asks to *see* the nickel. Bob seems not to want to show the nickel to Don, offering instead to *tell* Don about the coin: "I can tell you what it is," Bob says twice (60, 61). When Don suggests they look up the value of the coin in the blue book (what, until now, he seemed unwilling to do), Bob insists "the book don't *mean* shit" (62). Then Don finally seems to understand something: "Look, we're human beings. We can *talk,* we can negotiate, we can *this* . . . you need money? What do you need?" (62). Don's possible salvation is marked by his shift in emphasis away from a concern for discovering whether Bob is telling the truth or not, toward a concern for what Bob *needs.* In an ethical sense, Teach turns from an obsession with ethical chrematistics based on unbounded desire to a moral economy based on need. Teach then arrives to offer a kind of "last temptation" to Don, but this attempt at verbal manipulation is ultimately a desperate failure. Predictably, Teach works to exacerbate Don's deep-seated fear of ambiguity, and once again the symbol of that ambiguity is money: the second Buffalo nickel brought by Bob. This same nickel is of course also the emblem of Bob's apparent love and respect for Don: Bob, bleeding from the ear as a result of Teach's savagely hitting him with an object from Don's shop near the play's climax, finally admits he bought the nickel for Don with his own money. Bobby acted out of love and respect for Don, and Teach has no room in his worldview for this kind of behavior: "You people," he tells Don and Bob, "make my flesh crawl" (100).

What Don learns here is precisely what Teach can never know. Mamet is careful to point out a fundamental weakness engendered by Teach's constant use of language to manipulate: unlike Don and Bob, Teach never understands "talk" as "just talk," or as an attempt to be friendly, to establish community. In the first act, a seemingly innocent question of Don's (how Teach did in the poker game the night before) is interpreted by Teach as a kind of attack, or at least as meaning something else. Don has to explain "I'm just saying . . . for *talk*" (14). Similarly, when Don tries to engage in friendly chit chat about the weather, Teach takes his questions with an absurd literalness (20). Teach only understands talk as *useful* in getting what he wants by persuading others to act in a certain way. This is why Teach is so shocked to learn, as we all do by the end of the play, that all the planning he and Don have done in the course of the day was based on a lie: Bob had claimed that he saw the coin buyer (their intended victim) with a suitcase, apparently leaving on a trip, a claim he now reveals was false.

Ironically, while it is Don who is so troubled throughout the play by the inevitability of words (and money) to conceal, distort, and defer meaning, Teach is the one who explodes when Bob's lie is revealed: "There Is No Law. There Is No Right And Wrong. The World Is Lies. Every Fucking Thing [. . .] Every God-forsaken Thing [. . .] We all live like cavemen" (103). One supposes that it is not the lie *per se* that so shakes Teach, but the apparent unselfishness of the lie: Bob had nothing to gain from it except the respect and love of Don. And Teach's worldview, as we learn earlier in the play, is that civilization is essentially held together by *self-interest.* In one of the most quoted passages from any of Mamet's plays, Teach defines "free enterprise," that lynchpin of American culture, as "The freedom [. . .] Of the *individual* [. . .] To embark on Any Fucking Course that he sees fit [. . .] In order to secure his honest chance to make a profit" (72-3). "Without this," Teach goes on, "we're just savage shitheads in the wilderness [. . . .] Sitting around some vicious campfire" (73). The self-interested civilization Teach envisions – the civilization of laissez-faire capitalism[13] and of the depersonalized exchange envisioned by Simmel – is threatened, as Teach perceives, by the selflessness of Bobby. Moreover, Teach finds himself finally the victim of his own con. The very solipsism within which he tries to entrap Don – the view of the world as an endless language game completely divorced from the real – becomes finally Teach's own prison: "There is nothing out there," Teach proclaims as he tears apart Don's shop, "I fuck myself" (104).

Teach's reduction to solipsism and onanism powerfully reinforces the character's association with the very money that he tries to motivate Don to chase after. In the course of the play, money goes from being a symbol of monstrous self-generation – Shakespeare's "breed of barren metal" more plainly stated as a "fuckin' nickel" – to a token of fruitless masturbation. As Kurt Heinzelman points out, in addition to conceiving money as monstrously regenerative, Marx also sometimes portrayed money's seeming ability to produce itself from itself as onanistic. In this way Marx emphasized how money ultimately reduces even the commodities it would seem to represent to unimportant abstractions, and "enters now, so to say, into private relations with itself" (Marx qtd. in Heinzelman 177). Conceiving money as in this way onanistic allows Marx to emphasize that the laborer does not receive the benefit from money's seemingly generative properties, that in fact those properties of money ultimately take from the laborer even his own labor, "because the circulation of commodities through their money form has escalated the price of commodities beyond any wages that can possibly be tendered" (Heinzelman 177-8). In the climactic scene in Mamet's play, Teach personifies these very qualities of money, as he reduces the commodities in Don's shop to rubble and insists there is "nothing out there," i.e. nothing "outside" the economic realm that capitalism portrays as the real.

In Don's asking what Bob *wants* for the second coin, trying to establish an agreed-upon price based on the desires of the two negotiating parties, critic Thomas King reads the play's last word on the epistemological questions Mamet raises: "Look, we're human beings. We can *talk,* we can negotiate" (62). Through Don's seeking not the "objective" value of the coin but a value that would satisfy Bob's needs, King rightly notes, the play "teaches its audience that language is action in that its practical effect is more important than its referent" (545). The splitting of "talk" into action on the one hand and "just talk," or meaningless chit-chat, on the other – a division that occurs in nearly everything Mamet has written, as characters distinguish between "just talking" and " *really* talking" – is itself the reenactment of the anxiety over money at the heart of the discourse of naturalism, and which is still being obsessed over in the theatre today. By this logic, money must either be *only* paper and nothing else, or else it must somehow magically become the thing that it purports to represent. The idea of a paper money that signifies an agreed-upon value escapes this logic. The work of art, by the same logic, must either be a self-contained formal entity – the modernist flat canvas or the self-referential modern poem or play – or else it *becomes* the thing it purports to represent, as in the case of the modern method actor who strives not to imitate but to *re-create* a reality "from the inside" on the stage, or the naturalistic scene-designer who uses not facsimiles but *actual* furnishings to "recreate" the play's setting as realistically as possible.

It is difficult to read this play's critique of money's privileged claim to "reality" (as embodied by the treacherous Teach) without seeing in it also a critique of dramatic realism's similar claim to present "real life" on stage. Not only in his work but in his critical statements about his work, Mamet can be found struggling for ways to transcend the logic of naturalism. His contentious, at times paradoxical relationship with Stanislavski's theories of acting, and with their adapted form in the American "method," constitute one aspect of this struggle. Sometimes claiming he owes nearly everything to his reading of Stanislavski, Mamet nevertheless states in a 1997 interview that the actor who claims to conjure real emotions on stage is "lying" since "[t]here's nothing anyone can do to control his or her emotions" (Kane 205). In the same breath, Mamet denies the importance of "technique" to an actor, claiming he'd rather watch an enthusiastic beginner than a seasoned professional concerned with technique, and exhorts young actors to get on stage early so that they may begin mastering their craft (203-204). It is possible that Mamet is simply reveling in the con-man persona that so enthralls his artistic imagination. Whether or not this is the case, his paradoxical statements regarding an actor's "natural" ability and his need to master his craft, his calling for an "organic" theatre even as he distrusts emotion, resemble Don Dubrow's complicated statements on "skill" and "talent," and show Mamet struggling to complicate the simple, hard distinctions of the logic of naturalism.

Mamet's views on the relationship between the written text of the play and its performance further complicate matters, and here it is difficult to tell whether or not Mamet is himself ensnared within the logic of naturalism. Rejecting the idea that the actor "interprets" the play for the audience, Mamet claims instead that "the text reveals itself to the audience through the juxtaposition of the uninflected words, which the author wrote, and the moment-to-moment truthfulness of the actor" (Kane 202). While this feels like he is saying that meaning is created through a collaboration between playwright and actor, Mamet insists "I don't want to hear some actor's good ideas. I and you and everyone [. . .] has the capacity to go to a library and understand what the author meant" (202). The fantasy here of the author's meaning unproblematically encased within the text, stable, unchanging, self-evident, sounds like the naturalist fantasy of a world where things are what they seem, where money *is* the value it represents. Though ultimately, Mamet wants to transcend this logic. The text's stable meaning is married in performance to the actor's contribution: "the immediacy of the moment, [. . .] the organic moment-to-moment, back and forth, the Ping-Pong game of the unforeseen" (202). The metaphor is a strange but a telling one: a playwright more comfortable with the misdirection his work is subject to on the stage might have compared it, perhaps, to a game of billiards with its myriad, open-ended possibilities. The back-and-forth, relatively contained "Ping-Pong game of the unforeseen" is by contrast both an admission and a denial of this misdirection.

As with meaning, so with identity: this playwright whose trickster characters seem to reinforce the notion of identity as fluid, as performative, is nevertheless the artist who claims that American playwrights trying to apply the ideas of Artaud "is like black people trying to be white or white people trying to be black. There is a certain learned, habituated, perhaps even genetic cultural need for the rituals of the culture in which you exist and which is your culture" (Kane 62). That last sentence contains the essence of Mamet's wrestling match with the logic of naturalism, moving as it does from a concept of identity as "learned," to "habituated," and finally to "perhaps even genetic." Mamet is, I would argue, looking for a "third way" to think about identity that resists naturalism's distinction between nature and mimesis.

If, in *American Buffalo,* the misdirections, deceptions, and malleable truths of business and economic exchange constitute an aesthetic analogue to the same tendencies in language, it is perhaps unsurprising that Mamet's attitude toward business, like his attitude toward the dramatic art, like his attitude toward poker, involves contradictions. *American Buffalo,* like *Glengarry Glen Ross,* is obviously critical of American business. But as early as 1989, Mamet was able to describe business as an acceptable "male" activity: "Men get together to do business. Doing business is not devoid of fun. It gives us a sense of purpose" (*Some Freaks* 87). The "sense of purpose" business provides sounds at least a bit like Teach's view that the self-interest of what he calls free enterprise is a civilizing force, one that separates us from "savages."

In fact, Mamet has more specifically extolled the virtues of self-interest (and of business) in print. In his 2002 book-length reflection on his life in Vermont, *South of the Northeast Kingdom,* Mamet seems to call for a way of doing business that he associates with the values of both his adopted New England community and the Jewish heritage that has become an increasingly vital component of his identity in recent years. In contrast to the corporate model, the negotiating process of "the souk – indeed, of the antiques store, the auction, the farmers' market – is, finally, a mutual interrogation: a dialectic intended to reveal the truth." In Mamet's version of "doing business," what he calls the "self-respecting self-interest of the bazaar," the very components of economic life that so troubled the goldbugs and silver men – the indeterminacy of the sign, the negotiability of all prices, the unavoidable difference between face value and material value – are accepted, and perhaps even necessary, elements of the search for the truth (91). Paraphrasing a former Vermont governor's book *Justice in the Mountains,* Mamet explains that "Business is business, [. . .] and parties do business at arm's length, but there is, as part of the mountain ethos, a clear line between sharp practice and fraud. One may embellish and distract, but one may not lie" (*South* 78). Mamet goes on to associate this "Yankee" business ethic with a Jewish one, as he rescues the otherwise anti-Semitic term "rug merchant," translating what was once "seen as a non-Western (that is, a suspect, an unclean) way of doing business" into one morally superior to corporate capitalism, where all the power is on the side of the corporation, virtually none of it on the side of the buyer. This dialectic is, apparently, what is happening between Don and Bobby in the final act of *American Buffalo*. Unlike corporate capitalism, this dialectic happens in "a market unmoored by published and (seemingly) immutable prices" (90). In this dialectic, the "Western concept of Scout's Honor," itself, for Mamet, a lie intended to benefit those with power, is "supplanted by the no-fault understanding that each side will do business in its own best interest – and, therefore, that truth-in-utterance may neither be coerced nor enforced" (91). Instead of trying to "set a fair price in concert," the negotiating parties "set out each on his own. And no stigma is attached to dissimulation" (91).

Mamet's definition of business is fundamentally the same as his definitions of poker and of drama. In the hands of this playwright, business becomes a kind of sacrament. While Mamet seems to revel in teasing out the inherent contradictions of both economic life and its aesthetic manifestation in the naturalist theatre, he also seeks ultimately not to criticize but to redeem "business" and economic exchange. Finally *American Buffalo* seeks to justify both the money economy and the language economy by showing both as problematic but necessary systems of signification, and systems not inherently antithetical to the establishment of community between the male characters. Ultimately Don, like all of us, must learn to accept the inherent ambiguity of the sign, and love and trust other men in spite of this. At the same time, Mamet's redeemed economy is based on problematic, perhaps ultimately unsustainable distinctions such as that between "lying" and "dissimulation." Neither does Mamet explain how the quaint "self-interest" of the New England bazaar keeps from ultimately transforming into the rapacious self-interest of the corporate capitalism he decries.

Finally, a similarly strange, perhaps paradoxical mixture of respect for textual authority and desire for the open-endedness of signification is seen even in a very different sort of work by Mamet. In *Five Cities of Refuge,* his 2003 book of reflections on the Torah co-written with Rabbi Laurence Kushner, Mamet again insists on maintaining both textual authority and the free play of interpretation. In the introduction to that book Mamet writes:

> Our premise was that the biblical text always knew more than we did. A passage you suspect may be in error, mistaken, corrupt, incomplete or just plain wrong, offers only two real options: Either it's stupid or you are. If you choose the former, as many moderns do, you effectively cut yourself off from anything you don't agree with or understand. You place yourself above the text and can no longer be instructed or chastened by it.

Only a few lines later however, Mamet writes:

> This, of course, only raises the obvious problem of literalism. Jewish fundamentalism, it seems to us, differs from other literalist traditions in one important way. Others claim that because the biblical text is a vessel for God's word, it must be taken literally. Jews go further. If God is somehow in the biblical text, then not only must we revere the literal meaning of each word, we must assume that each word has infinite meaning. And that means that arguments are inescapable. Surely anything less would only trivialize sacred words.

If Mamet's seemingly paradoxical thinking on essence and sign is more artistically interesting than logically coherent, it is at least clear that the in imagining a method of meditation on the Torah that somehow respects and questions the authority of the text, as in imagining a Jewish/Yankee way of doing business that seeks to make room for the inevitable indeterminacy and supplementarity of both money and language and that simultaneously wants to believe in a "hard" authority behind both, as in imagining a theatrecraft where the ultimate authority of the text coincides with an ethic of improvisation, Mamet seeks a way of understanding identity – as well as art – as well as economics – as well as religion – that transcends the old either-or distinctions of essentialism or performativity, hard money or soft specie, the unquestioned logos or a meaningless, unending game of signification.

If the stylistic and philosophical tensions animating Mamet's work can be explained, at least partly, by the writer's rich and diverse literary heritage – one that includes the critique of positivism in expressionist plays of the 1920's like Rice's *The Adding Machine* and Treadwell's *Machinal* as well as the strong positivist ethos of what he refers to as the "Northern writers" (naturalist writers like Crane, Dreiser, and Cather, whom Mamet praises), a similar combination of diverse influences surely plays a role in the work of the next American playwright this study concerns itself with, who, like Mamet, investigates the intersection of economic life and racial/ethnic identity, and does so with at least one foot in the stream of American literary naturalism.

CHAPTER FIVE

"NEW MONEY" AND THE CIRCULATING BLACK BODY IN AUGUST WILSON'S *JOE TURNER'S COME AND GONE*

The second play, chronologically, in the ten-play body of work critics have called Wilson's "Century Cycle" (sometimes "Pittsburgh Cycle") of plays about the Black American experience in the twentieth century, *Joe Turner's Come and Gone* is set in 1911. Seth Holly and his wife Bertha run a boarding house in Pittsburgh that houses mostly black men and women fleeing the South following the disastrous Reconstruction period. A new boarder, Henry Loomis. has come to Pittsburgh with his daughter Zonia in search of Martha, Loomis's wife and Zonia's mother. Loomis was taken into forced labor in the notorious Joe Turner's chain gang for seven years, which separated him from Martha. With the help of another boarder named Bynum – a kind of shaman character – Loomis is eventually, though briefly, reunited with Martha and, more importantly, learns self-sufficiency and begins to recover from the trauma of his experience. Like other plays in the cycle, *Joe Turner's* makes use of both realist and mythic/magical realist dramatic modes. The play opened in 1986 at the Yale Repertory Theatre, then in 1988 at the Ethel Barrymore Theatre on Broadway, in a production directed by Lloyd Richards.

Wilson's exploration of money begins before the first word of *Joe Turner's* is even spoken, at least if we look at the printed editions of the play. Read carefully, the rather long prose passage that appears before the text-proper alerts us to a problem of perception that is rooted in economic thinking.[14] Setting the scene, Wilson transports us to 1911 Pittsburgh where the "sun falls out of heaven like a stone" and the "fires of the steel mill rage with a combined sense of industry and progress." The natural fire of the sun is thus replaced by the industrial/economic fire of the steel mill – a fire created by people, but one that seems somehow to have a will of its own. There is no mention of men or even people having a sense of progress: they are omitted altogether, as if the steel smelts itself and *it* has a sense of industry and progress. The natural world is thus replaced by the industrial/economic one; human agency is replaced by abstract industry. The rest of the description follows suit, seemingly ascribing agency to inanimate things and repressing/omitting people: “Barges loaded with coal and iron ore trudge up the river to the mill towns” and “return with fresh, hard, gleaming steel”; the “city flexes its muscles” (xvii). Only after all this description of the industrial/economic world in oddly human or natural terms do we get any sense of human agency: “Men,” we are told, “ throw countless bridges across the rivers, lay roads and carve tunnels” (xvii). Then after this one line we are right back to describing industrial/economic development as if it were nature: the “hills” through which men dig those tunnels are “sprouting with houses,” as if the houses *grow,* as if they are natural and independent of human efforts. In this introductory passage, Wilson employs a style reminiscent of the American naturalism that rose to prominence during the period when this play is set, the naturalism of Dreiser and Norris. Of course, with this style comes, inevitably, a way of seeing the world and humans' place in it. As in Dreiser's work, economic/industrial “forces” drive human action; as in Norris's, the economic is constructed as a kind of second nature. In this way Wilson's presentation of a thriving Pittsburgh in its industrial heyday is simultaneously a portrait of human alienation, of money's tendency to claim for itself an exclusive “reality” and reduce concrete human life to an abstraction.

In this introduction, Wilson does not say whether the “men” who throw bridges and dig tunnels are black or white, but we may presume they are largely the latter, since only *after* this description does the passage specifically mention “black men and women,” and these characters are described as *entering* the city to which we've already been introduced. The description of these black characters could not differ more markedly from all that purposeful activity associated with industrial (and white) Pittsburgh. The black men and women “wander into the city” (xvii). What's more, Wilson describes these wanderers as “[i]solated, cut off from memory, having forgotten the names of the gods and only guessing at their faces” (xvii). Thus does the play, at the very outset, work to emphasize the alienation of displaced black southerners in the years following Reconstruction. But this construction raises a question: if the industrial (white) milieu into which these men and women wander is already a site of human alienation, is there any hope of its offering them the self-sufficiency and sense of agency Wilson says they seek? These “marked men and women,” writes Wilson, are “seeking to scrape from the narrow, crooked cobbles and the fiery blasts of the coke furnace a way of bludgeoning and shaping the malleable parts of themselves into a new identity as free men of definite and sincere worth" (xvii). Here the naturalist rhetoric reveals a major – but critically undiscussed – difficulty at the heart of the play: how can an industrial economy that treats human life as an abstraction, that only values human beings as commodities, provide these men and women the identities they seek? Exactly what sort of "worth" can such a system endow them with? The naturalist rhetoric at work here does not allow for the kind of empowerment Wilson's characters need, and as long as the logic of that mode is at work, the best these characters can hope for is to move from one system of exploitation to another. If Wilson's characters are to achieve a "worth" that transcends their worth as laborers and commodities, the play will need to transcend this naturalistic mode.

Once the action of the play begins, we are introduced not to one of these isolated and wandering black men, but to Seth Holly, a black man born of free northern parents, a skilled maker and seller of pots and pans, and owner and operator (along with his wife Bertha) of a Pittsburgh boarding house. Throughout the play, Seth is associated with a certain type of "seeing" that is a key component of the logic of naturalism. In fact the play opens with Seth looking out a window and reporting on the doings of Bynum, and his first words (and thus the first words of the play) involve seeing and looking: "If that ain't the damnedest thing I seen. Look here, Bertha." In fact not only does Seth both report what he sees and order others to look, he even takes delight in seeing what he believes others cannot. His boarder Bynum, he says, is "down there on his hands and knees behind that bush looking all over for that pigeon and it on the other side of the yard. See it over there?" "Look at him," Seth goes on, "he still looking. He ain't seen it yet. All that old mumbo jumbo nonsense. I don't know why I put up with it" (1). Here, Seth's use of "mumbo jumbo" is telling, since the word refers both to an old African spiritual belief (likely derived from the Mandinka word "maamajomboo," according to the *OED)* and to nonsensical jargon used to mystify. The distance between the first and second meanings is more or less the distance between Bynum's and Seth's ways of "seeing." The play thus associates Seth's faith in the reliability of his empirical observations and his tendency toward a kind of positivist thinking with his rejection of the African spiritual traditions Bynum embodies. This is a crucial distinction since it is Bynum, as we will see, who allows Wilson to find a way out of the naturalist logic Seth's positivism demonstrates.

This is not to say that Seth's "seeing" has no value in the context of the play. Seth, after all, is the one who first correctly identifies Martha Pentecost as the wife Herald Loomis seeks; he sees a physical resemblance between Pentecost and Loomis's little girl Zonia. And Seth is correct, for example, when he insists that something "ain't right" with Herald Loomis, a judgment he repeatedly says he made as soon as he first laid eyes on Loomis (38, 60). The problem is that this businessman character relies so heavily – too heavily – on what he believes is his ability to get easily at the truth through a superficial observation. When Seth first meets Loomis, the stage directions tell us he *"stares at [him], sizing him up"* (14). What Seth concludes from this sizing up is that Loomis is not what he says he is. Loomis claims he was a Deacon in a church, but as Seth tells Bertha, "That's what he say. Do he look like a deacon to you?" (20). Of course Seth is wrong: Loomis was in fact a Deacon in a church until his enslavement by Joe Turner. In fact repeatedly in the play we see that what Seth "sees" is conditioned by his businessman's preoccupation with money. When Seth sees Loomis watching a church, he assumes mistakenly that he is "fixing to rob it" (33). The extent to which seeing and monetary accumulation are tied up in the character of Seth is nicely expressed when Seth complains about not getting a loan from local bankers to hire apprentices for his pot-making business: "They can't see that," Seth complains of the bankers. "Neither one of them can see that. Now, how much sense does it take to see that? All you got to do is be able to count. One man making ten pots is five men making fifty pots. But they can't see that" (43). In order to "see" like Seth one must possess a certain kind of "sense," one that sees other people as interchangeable commodities. In this way Wilson uses the character of Seth to undercut the positivism that formed the philosophical foundation of literary and dramatic naturalism by emphasizing the mediation of Seth's "seeing" by capitalism.

In fact, this notion of people as interchangeable is a major concern of the play. It is associated most closely with the characters of Seth and Selig the peddler and "people finder," and in both characters this propensity to see people as interchangeable is tied up with a certain disinterestedness associated with economic relations. Seth is fond of invoking "business" to explain his apparent disinterestedness in people as individuals, as when Molly tells him she occasionally likes to have a visitor in her room and Seth responds, "Your business is your business. I don't meddle in nobody's business," and earlier when he responds similarly to Jeremy's news that he and Mattie will share a room: "Your business is your business . . . but it's gonna cost her a dollar a week for her board. I can't be feeding nobody for free" (48, 44).

The economic roots of this view of people as interchangeable is made in a more disturbing manner through the character of the salesman and "people finder" Rutherford Selig. Immediately in the first scene Selig is associated with this view of people as interchangeable. When Bynum asks if Selig has seen the "Shiny Man" of his spiritual vision, Selig answers that the "only shiny man I saw was the Nigras working on the road gang with the sweat glistening on them" (8). Selig even advises Loomis that he'd be better off without a woman, and tells how he himself replaced his wife with a horse, the latter being "all a man needs" (40). But for associating a failure to see people as individuals with economic self-interest, these examples pale in comparison to Selig's description of his family's history in the "people finding" business. Selig explains that his great-grandfather "used to bring Nigras across the ocean on ships," a job that "set him well in pay" so he "settled in this new land and found him a wife of good Christian charity." Selig's father "used to find runaway slaves for the plantation bosses" and was "the best there was at it." Now that "Abraham Lincoln give you all Nigras your freedom papers," Selig's family finds "Nigras for Nigras." "Of course, it don't pay as much," admits Selig, "[b]ut the People Finding business ain't so bad" (41). This last statement especially, in which the middle passage, the hunting down of runaway slaves, and helping separated black families find one another are all monstrously equated under the term "business," and in which "bad" refers not to the ethics of any of these practices but to the *pay,* nicely demonstrates how money both replaces all other forms of value and how in doing so it conflates radically unlike things. As he does with Seth's "seeing," Wilson uses Selig's inability to make qualitative distinctions between slave trading, slave catching, and helping free black men and women locate lost loved ones to demonstrate the tragic limits of the positivistic view undergirding traditional naturalism, while also implicating economic thinking in this view.

Other characters in this play evince a tendency to view people as interchangeable to the point where it seems endemic. Molly Cunningham says of men, "One's just as good as the other if you ask me" (62). When Mattie is inconsolable at the loss of her man Jack Carper, Jeremy offers himself as a kind of temporary placeholder, as if one man is as good as another: "I'll be your man till he come," Jeremy explains (25). And the speed with which Jeremy's romantic interest transfers from Mattie to Molly only underscores the extent to which women are indistinguishable to him. As the money economy reduces all to least common denominator, so, apparently, does the sexual economy seem to erase difference between the characters.

Contrasted with Seth's and Selig's (and Jeremy's and Molly's) ways of seeing is Bynum's. Interestingly, Bynum, like Seth, claims to "see" Loomis's essence. In the second act, when Loomis asks how Bynum seems to know so much about him, the latter replies,

> I can tell from looking at you. My daddy taught me how to do that. Say when you look at a fellow, if you taught yourself to look for it, you can see his song written on him. Tell you what kind of man he is in the world. Now, I can look at you, Mr. Loomis, and see you a man who done forgot his song. (71)

At first glance this seems like the positivism that the play has already undercut through the characters Seth and Selig. But to understand the difference between the ways of seeing of Bynum on the one hand and Seth, Selig, Jeremy, and Molly on the other, we need to look at other statements by Bynum about seeing and identity. For instance, in the third scene of Act One, Bynum tries to teach Jeremy to appreciate women as more than just sexual beings:

> Now, you take a ship. Be out there on the water traveling about. You out there on that ship sailing to and from. And then you see some land. Just like you see a woman walking down the street. You see that land and it don't look like nothing but a line out there on the horizon. That's all it is when you first see it. A line that cross your path out there on the horizon. Now, a smart man know when he see that land, it ain't just a line setting out there. He know that if you get off the water to take a good look . . . why, there's a whole world right there. A whole world with everything imaginable under the sun. (46)

The more poetic kind of "seeing" Bynum tries to teach acknowledges empirical observation, and not just through vision: like seeing, "Touching's part of life," Bynum acknowledges, "It's in the world like everything else" (45). But on its own, according to Bynum, perception through the physical senses is not enough: as if in direct opposition to Selig's earlier statement regarding the replacement of his wife with a horse, Bynum tells Jeremy "[y]ou can lay your hand upside a horse or a cat, and that feels good too. What's the difference? When you grab hold to a woman, you got something there. You got a way of life kicking up under your hand" (45). Bynum's brand of "seeing" requires, in phenomenological terms, seeing the other person as a being-for-itself rather than just a being-in-itself. The object of one's gaze must be understood and respected as a subject in his or her own right. Bynum thus rejects the way of seeing of other characters that ultimately views people as objects meant merely to fulfill one's economic or sexual needs, and asserts instead a respectful awe in the face of the mystery that is another person. What Bynum advocates is, I believe, essentially what Heidegger called "the courage to stand amazed before the dawn" (31). Furthermore, Bynum acknowledges what the other characters do not: the extent to which one's own subjectivity is involved in what one "objectively" sees. In his nautical metaphor, the subject's own endless travel on the water greatly conditions what he perceives. He must "get off the water and take a good look" to see what the line on the horizon really represents – that is, he must have the courage and the faith to give himself over to this new object in order to truly see what it is. He must leave the sea and go to that line on the horizon. Thinking again about Bynum's supposed ability to "read" Loomis's character, it may be said that this reading requires that the reader imaginatively enter into the situation of the person he would read. As Bynum explains, he himself spent a period in search of his own "song." It is just this experience, combined with a willingness to empathize and a powerful imagination, that allows Bynum to "read" Joe Turner.

This meditation on seeing introduced by Bynum extends to the conversations between the two child characters of the play, the neighborhood boy Reuben and Loomis's daughter Zonia. In short scenes that punctuate the major action of the play, the two children engage in deceptively simple exchanges regarding the reading of other people, of one's self, and of the world at large. In Act Two Scene Four, for instance, Reuben reports to Zonia that he has seen Seth's mother, who has died. Zonia insists he "ain't seen nobody!" (79). But as the conversation continues it appears that Reuben has a more complex understanding of "seeing," one that goes beyond the purely empirical. He tells Zonia that he knows he will marry her some day because "I ask my grandpap how you know and he say when the moon falls into a girl's eyes that how you know" (83). As with Bynum's ability to "read" the world, which he learned from his father, Reuben's vision too begins with knowledge passed down from an earlier generation – in fact the knowledge in both instances comes from the same generation of black men. When Zonia asks if Reuben has seen the moon fall into her eyes, the boy's response recognizes a more complicated definition of "seeing": "That don't mean nothing 'cause I can't see it. I know it's there. Just the way you look at me sometimes look like the moon might have been in your eyes" (83). Reuben's response defines a more poetic, less empirical type of seeing and acknowledges Zonia's own subjectivity (the way she looks at him) as an irreplaceable part of what *he* sees, rejecting the positivistic fantasy of a Godlike subject simply perceiving an object. Zonia then responds in a manner that partakes of Seth's and Selig's strict empiricism: "That don't mean nothing if you can't see it. You supposed to see it." But Reuben persists, "Shucks, I see it good enough for me" (83).

The complexities of perception acknowledged in Bynum's and Reuben's statements are precisely what Seth fears. Seth's insistence on his ability to see everything and everyone, to "size them up," is evidence of this businessman's own anxiety regarding the unavoidable tendency of signs to deceive, and the involvement of money and economic "logic" in that gap between the symbolic and the real. In fact once in the play Seth uncharacteristically admits the deceptive nature of the visual sign. When, in Act One Scene Two, Bertha suggests that Loomis does not *look* like the kind of man that would rob a church, Seth insists that looks cannot tell us much. "I ain't saying how he look," says Seth, "It's how he do. Anybody liable to do anything as far as I'm concerned" (33). Then he doubts that Herald Loomis is even his real name: "Anybody can tell anybody anything about what their name is. That's what you call him . . . Herald Loomis. His name is liable to be anything" (33).

Like other businessmen characters in the American realist/naturalist dramatic tradition, Seth is ultimately repressing a deep distrust of signs. He would "look one in the eye" and "size them up," even as he frets that appearances tell him nothing. We have seen this same phenomenon in Mamet's *American Buffalo,* where Don's anxieties concerning the lack of a "hard" distinction between talk and action, his inability to either engage in or speak of financial transactions, and his planned theft of the buffalo nickel legitimately purchased all speak to his inability to think outside a naturalist logic embodied by Teach, a character who both terrifies and tantalizes Don with the message that while Don can deal only in the soft currency of representations that have no relation to the gold standard of the real, he (Teach) somehow has transcendental access to that real. In Miller's *Death of a Salesman,* Willy Loman evinces a similar distrust of signs, which leads him to fetishize his brother Ben's promise of diamonds, a value one can "hold in the hand" as opposed to the empty promise of his own "appointments." In Seth's case, when his wife Bertha suggests that maybe it is Martha Pentecost who gave them a false name (which is more true than what Seth thinks), Seth dismisses this on the basis that "Martha's a good Christian woman. This fellow here look like he owe the devil a day's work and he's trying to figure out how he gonna pay him. Martha ain't had a speck of distrust about her the whole time she was living here" (34). This passage is remarkable for the way it demonstrates simultaneously a reliance on empirical observation (how Loomis *looks*) and a claim to knowledge of Martha's essentially "good," "Christian" essence.

When Seth remarks that Martha Pentecost has not had "a speck of distrust about her," he seems to be referring now not to the visual but to the linguistic sign. Seth's statement is ironic given the fact that repeatedly in the play he betrays an anxiety over the tendency of language – especially spoken language – to deceive just as troublingly as appearances do. The financial viability of Seth's boarding house, we are reminded more than once, relies heavily on the house's reputation – relies, that is, on a public kind of "talk" that Seth perceives as worryingly beyond his control. In the first scene of the play Seth lectures Jeremy, who has just spent a night in jail, that "everybody" knows his house is "respectable," and that is why he will not "put up with no foolishness" (13). When Martha, as usual, asks Seth to be reasonable, Seth insists, "I ain't gonna have folks talking" (13). Coupled with Seth's anxiety over the talk of others are his attempts to control situations through enacting or withholding talk of his own. Seth, after all, knows where Loomis's wife Martha is all along, but decides to keep this information from Loomis (36). And there are several instances in the play of Seth using talk in successful negotiations. When, for example, Loomis balks at Seth's asking for extra money to house his daughter, arguing that she sleeps in the same room, Seth asks rhetorically, "Do she eat off the same plate?" (42), and Loomis hands over the extra dollar. Seth is similarly canny in his negotiations in the beginning of the play with Selig, who both supplies Seth with sheet metal and then peddles the pots, pans, and dustpans that result from Seth's labor. Seth convinces Selig to sell him the sheet metal for sixty percent less than Selig asked for (fifteen cents a piece versus the twenty-five cents Selig says they originally agreed on) (7). Both Seth's skillful use of "talk" and his strategic silences demonstrate this character's keen appreciation of and understandable anxiety over language and the gap it opens between the symbolic and the real, though he actively tries to suppress this knowledge.

When Seth is not able to control the talk of others, he denies the value of talk by insisting on a hard distinction between talk and action, the symbolic and the real. Playing dominoes with Bynum in the second act, Seth chides his opponent for chattering and singing while they are playing: "Come on and play," says Seth. "You ain't doing nothing but talking. I got a hundred and forty points to your eighty. You ain't doing nothing but talking. Come on and play" (68). Characteristically, Seth would make a hard distinction between talk and action, the symbolic and the real. There are two more examples of this in the first act. The first involves Seth's skepticism about Selig's supposed ability to find people. "He talk all that," claims Seth, "but unless he get lucky and knock on her door he can't find her. That's the only way he find anybody. He got to get lucky. But I know just where she at" (38). Here Seth characteristically devalues the "talk" of others and claims for himself a kind of direct knowledge of the truth. In a second example of this tendency of Seth's, a dispute arises between Seth and Bertha over when exactly Martha came to stay at the boarding house. Bertha claims Martha arrived after Bynum, in fact that she came specifically to seek out Bynum's help. Seth, however, remembers differently, and claims Martha was already living at the house when Bynum arrived. In this disagreement, Seth interestingly opens a gap between his own empirical observation and the "talk" of Bertha. "You can say what you want," says Seth, "I know the facts of it" (36). The argument is eventually settled in Bertha's favor – Bynum did in fact arrive before Martha, and the "facts" Seth claims exclusive access to are not what he thought they were. Bertha is only finally able to convince Seth that he is wrong by reminding him about another boarder who still owes Seth $200 – further evidence of the mediation of what Seth calls the "facts" by his own businessman's preoccupation with money.

Seth's fantasy of closing the gap between symbols and reality is, as critic Jean-Joseph Goux has pointed out, the fantasy of gold money. Seth longs for what Goux suggests the American gold-money of the nineteenth and early twentieth centuries promised but could not possibly deliver: the erasure of difference between the real and the symbolic, a substance that *is* the value it *represents*. Goux writes, "At once the ideal measure of value, the symbolic instrument of exchange, and the real means of reserve, gold-money brought together the functions of archetype, of token, and of treasure into a single object." Yet with the advent of representative money (paper, then credit cards, then electronic money), the "three functions have come asunder" (114).

The action of *Joe Turner's* takes place just eleven years after the establishment of a gold standard for the U.S. Dollar. And it is worth noting that the debates surrounding gold and its relation to American money have had a close association with American rhetoric around the idea of race. Historian Michael O'Malley notes that gold-standard debates about a stable currency and a natural (or, alternately, an inflated) value were powerfully involved in constructions of "race" in America during the Civil War and the pivotal period of Reconstruction. During the War, the Union issued $450 million in those threateningly "soft" greenbacks and, in 1863, passed the National Banking Act, which taxed the various state bank notes circulating at the time out of existence and effectively established a uniform currency for the first time in America (*Face Value* 378). Almost from the time of its issue, the paper money began depreciating relative to gold. In the metallist rhetoric of the time, gold and silver were associated with "natural" value, the greenbacks considered of artificial or "inflated" value. In 1865 Treasury Secretary Hugh McCulloch said of the "natural" value of gold and silver, "I myself have no more doubt that these metals were prepared by the Almighty for this purpose, than I have that iron and coal were prepared for the purposes for which they are being used" (qtd. in O'Malley 378). After the war, the funding of the Freedmen's Savings Bank with greenbacks further associated the construction of "artificial" paper money with the construction of "artificial" citizens out of former slaves. "Diluting the money supply" was equated with "dilut[ing] the nation's blood, and elevating the freedmen depreciated the value of whiteness" (381). At the same time, writes O'Malley, "[f]rom the greenback perspective, a legal declaration of equality, an expression of cultural or political authority, could bring about equality just as a congressional declaration of the value of paper money could give the paper value" (379). The greenback, in other words, was seen as either a fictive imitation of natural value, or as an instrument that helped create the value it represented, just as calling former slaves citizens helped make them such. The debates around gold and paper money during the Reconstruction period are perhaps the most powerful evidence we have of the deep interconnection between money, symbolic, and racial economies – evidence that, as Michael Germana points out, "The meaning of words, the value of money, and the significance of race all fluctuate within economies of difference" that are deeply involved with one another (1).

Wilson's play cleverly teases out money's involvement in the construction of race through its repeated association of the term "mark" or "marked" with the play's black characters. The prologue to the play, as we have mentioned, describes its characters as "marked men and women" (xvii). Here the old racist idea of black people as carrying the "mark of Cain" intersects with another definition of "mark": for centuries the term was used widely in western Europe to refer to a specific quantity of gold or silver, and even today refers specifically to a German unit of currency (a definition with which Wilson, whose father was a German immigrant to America, was surely familiar). The men of *Joe Turner's* are thus doubly marked: once by their race and once again by their status as commodities. Both these marks threaten to subsume their identities, to "mark" them as interchangeable "black" men and as interchangeable commodities.

The notion of a marked man (or woman) is, in both senses just discussed, at the very heart of naturalism's anxiety over the slipperiness of the sign, its need to perceive from the "outside" the *essential* value of a currency or a person, its fantasy of erasing the gap between the symbolic and the real. This is the cultural logic of Seth and Selig. Henry Loomis rightly fears this logic, and this fear leads to his mistaking Bynum's knowledge of his past for Seth's simplistic insistence on an ability to "size" one up. After Bynum explains that he can tell Loomis is "one of Joe

Turner's niggers," Loomis explodes, "You lie! How you see that? I got a mark on me? Joe Turner done marked me to where you can see it? You telling me I'm a marked man" (71). As a force beyond one's control that nevertheless fixes one's identity and therefore more or less decides one's fate, the mark bears strong resemblance to the Calvinist idea of election so influential in American Puritan culture. Nathaniel Hawthorne, by the mid-nineteenth century, already recognized the enduring nature – and the danger – of this Puritan belief: that titular letter on Hester's breast is, among other things, evidence of a powerful Calvinist wish to make her "outside" reflective of her "inside" or spiritual state. By the turn of the twentieth century the naturalism of Crane and Dreiser inscribed race and ethnicity as major factors fixing the identity of its characters, and it did this under the assumed authority of a "realist," even "scientific" gaze.

It is this obsession with *essences* – born of an anxiety over the tendency of appearances to deceive – that drives American literary naturalism's deterministic view, or at the very least drives the genre's preoccupation with questions regarding human freedom and its limits. For Wilson, whose style is heavily indebted to American literary naturalism, the challenge becomes how to find a way for his disenfranchised men and women – so often the object of the naturalist literary gaze – to have agency. As with so much else in this play, the key to how Wilson accomplishes this is the character Bynum. As a shaman, or what another character refers to as one of the "bones people," Bynum functions as a conduit between the physical world of the play's characters and the mythic world of his own and others' (especially Loomis's) visions. As a character, Bynum also exists at the intersection of Wilson's naturalism and the play's mythic or, in the judgment of some critics, it's magic realist elements. Marc Maufort has written about the way Wilson's play makes use of magic realism in order to designate what Jeanne Delbaere calls a "'fracture in the real,' a sense of crisis the imagery of Wilson's dramaturgy undoubtedly brings about" (174). In this way Wilson uses magic realism to try to build a bridge from the positivistic, naturalist logic that dominates the dramatic tradition from which he emerges toward some new aesthetic and philosophical vision. Maufort notes Wilson's use of a specific type of magic realism, what Delbaere labels "grotesque realism," a mode "which tends to even further distort and amplify reality" (256). Delbaere notes that grotesque realism is employed "for any sort of hyperbolic distortion that creates a sense of strangeness through the confusion or interpenetration of different realms like animate/inanimate or human/animal" (qtd in Maufort 256). In *Joe Turner's,* this mode appears most prominently in the visions of the shaman Bynum and the wanderer Joe Turner. In Bynum's vision, a "shiny man" leads him to a place where "everything look like it was twice as big as it was." Eventually Bynum's father appears, but with enormous hands and mouth. Bynum's father tells his son that once he sees a second "shiny man" he can die happy, and he also gives him a new sense of his own identity or (in a powerful metaphor of the play), his "song." The identity Bynum's father helps Bynum to see involves not only how he views himself but, inseparably from this, a service he will provide to others: Bynum has "the binding song," a power to help other wanderers reconnect (9-10). Loomis's vision similarly makes use of grotesque realism. Conflating the Middle Passage with Ezekiel's vision from the Old Testament and also African spiritual traditions, Loomis's vision contains bones rising up and walking on water – water that is "bigger than the whole world." These walking skeletons eventually sink into the water, then a giant wave rises and washes them up on dry land, whereupon they acquire flesh and black skin (53).

Through both Bynum's and Loomis's visions, *Joe Turner's* marks what Delbaere calls a fracture in the real. More specifically, the play disrupts the positivist fantasy at he heart of aesthetic naturalism by foregrounding the very gap between the symbolic and the real that naturalism would repress. Moreover, each vision looks for a way of transcending the logic of naturalism by emphasizing the limits of language. The fullness of Bynum's vision cannot be communicated by language; Bynum says that his father showed him something ""I ain't got words to tell you. But if you stand to witness it, you done seen something there" (10). Similarly, Loomis precedes his attempt to relate his vision with the caveat, "Herald Loomis done seen some things he ain't got words to tell you" (52-3). In fact when Loomis first hears the African "juba" chanting of the other boarders that leads to his relating his vision, he is initially unable to form words and begins to *"speak in tongues and dance around the kitchen,"* according to Wilson's stage directions. Loomis and Bynum both mark the limits of naturalism and even the limits of language in the work of constructing a narrative that can begin to heal a traumatized black American populace in the years after the Civil War and the period of Reconstruction, that can begin to offer these men and women a connection with a lost past and also a way forward.

Perhaps the strongest statement in the play regarding the limits of language occurs in Act Two Scene Five, which concludes with Seth's wife Bertha's wordless dance through the kitchen. Wilson's stage directions tell us Bertha *"moves about the kitchen as though blessing it and chasing away the huge sadness that seems to envelop it."* It is *"a dance and demonstration of her own magic, her own remedy that is centuries old and to which she is connected by the muscles of her heart and the blood's memory"* (87). As in the visions of Bynum and Loomis, here in Bertha's dance the mythic or magic realist penetrates the real of the play, and as in those visions, the limits of language are foregrounded. Furthermore, this emphasis on the performative in Wilson's play resists the logic of naturalism in a more radical way than the prose writing of his naturalist forebears could possibly have done.

Like the other playwrights discussed here, Wilson is striving toward some new, post-naturalist way of thinking about identity in America – in Wilson's case, black identity – or, more precisely, some way of thinking that shares some of naturalism's emphasis on the body and its highly conditional view of free will, but also adopts a more postmodern stance by acknowledging the interpenetrability of the symbolic and the real. Bynum's lecture to Jeremy on how to "see" a woman was one such attempt at this new way of thinking. A second is Bynum's philosophy of free will. He has a certain power to "bind" people together, he says, but he can only do so when the people in question are *meant to* find each other. Similarly, he can help people find their "song" – their identity – but that song must come from deep inside that person, not from Bynum. In this way Wilson would seem to retain elements of naturalism's highly determined universe but also to imagine a sort of agency that works within that determined world. At play's end, Henry Loomis is finally free of the trauma of his time on Joe Turner's gang, but that freedom is somewhat ambiguous: he is *"free from any encumbrance other than the workings of his own heart and the bonds of the flesh"* (94). Hasn't it been the workings of his own heart that have kept him in search of his wife for so long? In what way will things be different for him now? These questions are not answered by Wilson's play. What we are left with instead is one last reference to money in the figuring of identity. Earlier in the play Bynum described the "shiny man" of his spiritual vision as "shining like new money" (9). Now at the play's end Bynum returns to the term, describing the newly self-sufficient Henry Loomis – in the last words of the play – as "shining like new money!" The metaphor is a strange one, given the play's exploration of money's involvement in a logic of naturalism that has "marked" black men as determined bodies and as commodities (94). It is perhaps best read ultimately as a pragmatic vision, one that sees a kind of structured agency within what it recognizes as the (at least in 1911) inescapable realities of economies of race, language, and money that will continue to condition our thinking about identity in America, even to the present day.

But the term may represent something more than this. The very idea of "new money" is a kind of paradox, since it is precisely the conventionality of money that gives it value: that is, money must be recognized and its value agreed to by all parties to an economic transaction for it to be useful. Therefore the notion of "new money," like the notion (in *American Buffalo*) of "real Classical money," like the humanized/commoditized salesman of Miller's play, is another instance of the uncanny (or, as Delbaere calls it, a "fracture in the real"). As such it has the power to expose the essentially *constructed* nature of that seemingly "natural" economic activity Wilson describes in the prologue to the play, the radical potential to at least point a way past the monstrosity of the situation the play describes. This role of economic, racial, and linguistic economies in the construction of the "real" is the primary subject of the final playwright under study here.

CHAPTER SIX

MAKING IT "REAL": VERBAL, SEXUAL, AND REPRODUCTIVE ECONOMIES IN SUZAN-LORI PARKS'S *TOPDOG/UNDERDOG* AND "RED LETTER" PLAYS

In an essay entitled "Possession," American playwright Suzan-Lori Parks quotes from John S. Mbiti's *African Religions and Philosophy,* concerning the "living dead":

> They belong to the time period of the Zamani [past] and by entering individuals in the Sasa [present] period, they become our contemporaries. The state of possession and mediumship is one of contemporarizing the past, bringing into human history the beings essentially beyond the horizon of present time. (qtd in "Elements" 5)

In a series of groundbreaking plays, Parks has repeatedly revisited this theme of the relation of the living to the dead, the present to the past. In her Pulitzer Prize-winning 2001 play *Topdog/Underdog,* the two brothers who make up the work's entire cast of onstage characters embody Parks's complex notion of these relationships. Two African American men sharing a cramped one-room apartment with no running water, the brothers only happen to be named Lincoln and Booth – names given them by their father as a "joke" (29). The apparently arbitrary relationship of the characters to their given names notwithstanding, Lincoln, the older brother, ekes out a living portraying his Presidential namesake (complete with whiteface makeup) in an arcade, where customers pay a fee to pretend to shoot him and where he pretends to die, over and over again. Younger brother Booth ultimately and with more tragic consequences lives up to his name by *actually* shooting and killing Lincoln by play's end. Thus do the brothers give disturbing meaning to the notion of "contemporarizing the past." The simultaneously arbitrary and compelling relation of these characters to their names is part of what emerges in *Topdog/Underdog* as an exploration of the complex relation of the apparent to the real, the performative to the authentic, and the past to the present. As in the other plays in this study, money and the sale/confidence-trick are at the center of that exploration in Parks's play.

Looming large on the horizon of the brothers' own shared past are two almost identical financial transactions. One day during the boys' adolescence their mother gave $500 to Booth and left forever. Two years later, the boys' father gave $500 to Lincoln and was never seen by his sons again. A marker of the dismemberment of the family, money also paradoxically holds forth the promise of reunification, through the brothers' attempt to create a kind of simulacrum of the traditional American nuclear family with Lincoln as the sole "bread-winner," and through the younger brother Booth's desperate attempts to convince Lincoln to go into "business" with him as a three-card monte hustler – a life Lincoln once lived and now desperately tries to resist.

In the struggle for power at the center of *Topdog/Underdog,* Booth needs to believe that his skill with the confidence game of three-card monte equals or even exceeds that of his older brother Lincoln, a one-time master of the con who has given up the game after the violent death of one of his "crew." Yet evidence suggests Booth lacks Lincoln's innate skill: where the older brother seems to possess a natural talent for the game, Booth's moves with the cards are "studied and awkward"; he throws the cards, Parks's stage directions tell us, *"in an awkward imitation of his brother"* (11, 83). Booth similarly tries to imitate what Lincoln calls his "patter," or the rapid-fire speech meant to both entice and confuse the confidence artist's "mark;" yet Booth, as Lincoln attempts to tell him, is trying to master only the superficial or "outward" signs of a game that requires a much deeper understanding. "Theres 2 parts to throwing thuh cards," explains Lincoln. "Both parts are fairly complicated. Thuh moves and the grooves, thuh talk and thuh walk, the patter and the pitter pat, thuh rap and thuh flap: what yr doing with yr mouth and what yr doing with yr hands"(79).

Thus does Lincoln bring up the paradoxical distinction that haunts the other plays under discussion here, and that represents one way of inscribing the logic of naturalism: that between saying and doing, word and action, "talk" and "walk." Booth, in keeping with other aspects of his character (as we'll see), seems to believe that mastering one of these aspects of the game is enough: "I got thuh words down pretty good," he tells Lincoln, who futilely repeats his point: "You need to work on both" (79). For Parks as for her character Lincoln, the very distinction between word and action is the beginning of an error. Of the lack of stage directions in her drama she has written that the "action goes in the line of dialogue instead of always in a pissy set of parentheses. *How* the line should be delivered is contained in the line itself" ("Elements of Style" 15-16). Booth never understands this interdependence of language and action – the heart of the lesson Lincoln would teach him – and persists in the false distinction to the very end of the play.

In fact, Booth's approach to three-card monte is of a piece with a general approach to life he evinces throughout the play, one that values word over action, symbol over referent, appearance over essence. Something as instrumental as a telephone is valued by Booth not for its use-value (as one would normally think of it), but for its importance as a symbol in the dating market. Being able to give your phone number to a woman, according to Booth, tells her "3 things: 1) you got a home [. . .] 2) that you is in possession of a telephone and a working telephone number," which in turn sends the signal that "you together enough to pay yr bills" (3). Finally, the phone number offered to a woman is "telling her that its cool to call if she should so please, that is, that you aint got no wife or wife approximation on the premises" (36-7). Similarly, Booth places great value on clothing as symbol. Having given Lincoln a suit he stole, he advises his brother that wearing it will "make you feel good and when you feel good yll meet someone nice" (34). In each of these examples Booth's apparent view is that the symbolic (the "talk") creates (rather than also reflecting) the real (the "walk"). In this attitude Booth sometimes resembles Miller's Willy Loman, who teaches his sons that a smile and the right "appearance" will bring great success, as well as the young Biff Loman, who needs reminding by Bernard that writing the name of the college he wishes to attend on his athletic shoes will not make up for his poor academic performance (Miller 29). At the same time, Booth is of course generally right to consider the way signs are involved in the construction of that which they represent. No one would deny that dressing so that one "looks good" may make one feel confident, which, through any number of situations, could lead to a material improvement in one's situation. In the same way, Willy Loman is basically right that an attention to one's "appearance" is one important part of materially improving one's lot, and not only in the world of sales. It is these characters' oversimplification of the relation between the real and the symbolic that is being criticized in Miller's and Parks's plays, their failure to see that these categories are dialectically involved in one another. A belief that controlling appearances always allows one to control the real appears here as a kind of naïve postmodernism, as dangerously misleading as a naïve essentialism that sees the symbolic as always and only a direct reflection of the materially real.

Two further elements in Booth's life demonstrate his apparent belief that an attention to signifiers is all he needs to affect the real. One is his attempt to change his name. Early in the play he orders Lincoln to call him by a new moniker: "3 Card" (23). Despite Lincoln's repeated attempts to teach Booth that becoming a three-card monte hustler takes much practice and understanding, Booth seems to believe that once he calls himself one, he will be one. He even threatens that anyone who will not call him by this new name "gets a bullet," demonstrating Booth's desperate attempts to control the real by controlling signifiers (23).

Finally Booth's naïve emphasis on signs is evident in his relationship – or lack of one – with the never-seen Grace. All the failed strategies Booth employs to win Grace involve style over substance, including attention to clothes and to the look of his apartment as well as a ring that is "diamond-esque" but "looks just as good as the real thing" (14). Grace herself, in fact, is apparently dealing in outward deceptions of a sort, as she studies "cosmetology" (47). Even in the sexual act (one, we learn, that probably never occurred), the visual sign is emphasized: Booth insists on having sex with Grace in front of a mirror – as Lincoln says, "So you could see her" (46). Booth's obsessive need to control signs is the result of the character's intimate knowledge of and deep fear of the often arbitrary and deceptive relationship between signs and the real. Booth's constant suspicions regarding Grace and other men are symbolic of his anxiety regarding the tendency of signs to deceive.

In fact Booth's sex life is even more strictly visual than his (probably imagined) encounter with Grace would suggest, for a recurring theme in the play is Booth's interest in pornographic magazines and masturbation. In Scene Three, after accusing Booth of lying about having sex with Grace that evening, Lincoln reveals that he found "like 100" such magazines, along with biological evidence of Booth's proclivity for masturbation, under the younger brother's bed (49). Booth's interest in pornography is crucial to understanding the character's symbolic importance in the play, since it not only relates to his general preference for signs over reality, but also underscores the relation of this tendency to an attitude toward money.

In his important work *Symbolic Economies,* Jean-Joseph Goux relates the fetishization of the penis as "general equivalent" of sexual desire to the fetishization of money as general equivalent in economic life. Summarizing Marx's geneology of money in *Capital,* Goux remarks that in a money economy, the commodity chosen to function as money is "excluded from immediate consumption (and, as Marx emphasizes, gold and silver, as money, are in reality completely barred from use in immediate production)" (36). The commodity chosen to become money is excluded from the universe of other commodities, even as it makes all else into a commodity. In the same way, writes Goux, "the choice of the penis as the general equivalent is *the means* of excluding it from immediate use. The phallus's function as general equivalent *forbids* its immediate use. It can and must function only in a relationship of exchange or circulation" (37). "Thus," writes Goux, "promoting the phallus to the rank of general equivalent prohibits, first of all, immediate use (masturbation), and second, immediate exchange (incest)" (37-8).

If one would argue that Goux makes too much of the symbolic relationship between the penis and money as general equivalents in systems of exchange, it must be remembered that Parks herself makes this connection clear through the speech of Booth. Booth explains, for instance, that he masturbates because he *cannot afford* to enter into a real sexual relationship. "If I wasnt taking care of myself by myself," he explains, "I would be out there running around on thuh town which costs cash that I dont have so I would be doing worse: I'd be out there doing who knows what, shooting people and shit. Out of a need for unresolved sexual release" (49). Earlier in the play, Booth muses that if Lincoln would go back to hustling cards, he "could afford to get laid" and "Grace would be all over [Booth] again" (24-5). And again near the play's end, Booth speaks of sex with Grace as an economic transaction: "She gonna walk in here looking all hot and shit trying to see how much she can get me to sweat, how much she can get me to give her before she gives me mines" (72). If, as Goux writes, economic and sexual exchange prohibit "immediate use" of the penis/money, Booth's preference for masturbation over sexual intercourse may be seen as part of the same logic which necessitates the character's repression of money.

In addition to the "immediate use" of masturbation, Goux names incest as a taboo involving "immediate exchange" of the penis. In fact the only sexual exchange we think Booth likely engaged in occurred before the action of the play, when he slept with his brother's wife, Cookie – an action that, strictly speaking, does not fit the definition of incest but is close enough to be symbolically significant. Even more interesting, Booth's memories of his mother involve him in a kind of symbolically incestuous relationship with her. In Scene Six, Booth confesses to knowing of his mother's adulterous relationship before she abandoned her sons. In a scene foreshadowing his own fascination with pornography, Booth remembers "watching them" have sex without being seen himself, and somehow both sharing and not sharing this secret with his mother: at dinner later "she would look at me," recalls Booth paradoxically, "like she didn't know that I knew but she was asking me not to tell nohow. She was asking me to – oh who knows" (104). Unsurprisingly for this character deeply suspicious of signs he cannot control, this imagined moment of understanding between himself and his mother occurs without words.

Booth's role as unseen spectator coupled with the unspoken secret he imagines he and his mother shared involves him in a kind of symbolically incestuous relationship with his mother. What's more, money is at the heart of Booth's memories of his mother. Booth twice repeats that his mother's paramour was fond of saying "I aint made of money," and he recalls a scene in which his mother becomes pregnant and the man refuses to pay for an abortion (104-5). Two months later, Booth recalls, his mother, having somehow terminated the unwanted pregnancy, gives Booth money and leaves him forever: "she had my payoff – my *inheritance* – she had it all ready for me. 500 dollars in a nylon stocking" (105). The "payoff" Booth's mother made to him before abandoning him certainly gives Booth reason to have an uneasy relationship with money. The personal – even sexual – nature of the object Booth's mother uses to wrap the money – an object that itself calls to mind the stocking as emblem of sexual exchange in Miller's masterpiece – further underscores the close relation between money and sexuality for Booth.

Moreover, Booth's memories of his mother repeatedly invoke the trope of monstrosity, or at least of unnatural generation. Booth's mother's extra-marital affair leads to an unwanted pregnancy – an instance of sexual generation that threatens to disrupt the nuclear family. In Aristotle's economic terms, the *krema* of limitless desire threatens to destroy the *oikos* of household economy. The tragic solution to this problem is money, in the form of a payment for an abortion that Booth's mother must request from the father of the unwanted child. That father's answer is that he is not "made of money." Ultimately Booth's mother *is* in a sense made of money, as she disappears and leaves in her stead a monstrous version of herself: a sum of money wrapped in her stocking. The mother's ungenerative sex then leaves a legacy in Booth's lifelong onanism.

Here it is important that just as Booth fails (or refuses) to enter into sexual "exchange," opting instead for masturbation, neither does he enter into economic exchange. While Lincoln earns and (as we'll see) spends money continuously, Booth does neither. Booth refuses to work, apparently associating holding a "steady job" with his parents' breaking up and leaving their children:

> Like neither of them couldnt handle it no more. She split than he split. Like thuh whole family mortgage bills going to work thing was just too much. And I dont blame them. You dont see me holding down a steady

> job. Cause its bullshit and I know it. I seen how it cracked them up and I aint going there. (72)

Though Booth is given more than a fair share of Lincoln's income every payday, he somehow avoids spending it. In the course of the play, Booth steals clothing, magazines, food, and fancy tableware. We neither see nor hear of his purchasing anything. Like the junkshop owner Don Dubrow in Mamet's *American Buffalo,* who spends the entire play scheming to get back a coin that was legitimately purchased from him, Booth appears here as a species of the miser; his fortune cookie, early in the play (part of a meal his brother Lincoln pays for), reads "Waste not want not" (22). As with Don Dubrow, Booth's aversion to spending is symptomatic of the character's repression of money and the anxiety over appearances and authenticity money symbolizes. The great symbol of Booth's attempt to "escape" the money economy is that $500 in a stocking given him by his mother as she left him. Unlike Lincoln (who received the same amount from his father and who spent his), Booth has never spent his money. In fact he never even took it out of the stocking and counted it. When, early in the play, Booth refers to his still having his inheritance, Lincoln points out that, in effect, his inheritance is *not* money as long as he refuses to do anything with it: "Thats like saying you dont got no money cause you aint never gonna do nothing with it so its like you dont got it" (21-22). And of course it is Lincoln's attempt to cut open the stocking and verify the existence of the $500 that propels Booth toward his last violent act at play's end. Thus does Booth exist in a kind of sexual and economic limbo, represented by that uncounted $500 wrapped in his mother's stocking. Booth spends neither his sexual nor his economic power, but denies both: his money is wrapped and uncounted, his semen lies fallow on the magazines Lincoln finds underneath his bed. Money is brought into the small apartment that is the play's sole setting through Lincoln's work, but no money, if Booth has anything to do with it, flows out. In fact, *nothing at all* flows out: Lincoln points out twice that the apartment has no running water, and at one point we witness the older brother urinate in a cup, which he then places in a corner of the apartment (59). Not even bodily emissions may be "spent."

Given the play's association between money and bodily emissions, it is not insignificant that Lincoln – not Booth – is the character who urinates on stage in this play. Where Booth is loath to spend any money, Lincoln represents the opposite extreme, and greatly enjoys spending. He has not, like Booth, saved his $500 "inheritance" but has long since spent it. When he first appears in the play Lincoln announces that he has just "[b]ought drinks at Luckys. A round for everybody" (16). When he is finally fired from his job at the arcade near the end of the play, Lincoln takes a severance package of a week's pay and "blew it. Spent it all" (70). When Booth asks "On what?" Lincoln responds, "—Just spent it." (70). It is unimportant on what he spent it; the act of spending itself is where Lincoln finds power. "It felt good," he explains, "spending it. Felt really good. Like back in thuh day when I was really making money" (70).

With regard to Lincoln's spending, the similarities and differences between Lincoln's and Booth's methods of receiving their "inheritance" are interesting. Where the boys' mother gives Booth "5 hundred-dollar bills rolled up and tied up tight in one of her nylon stockings," the father gives Lincoln "10 fifties in a clean handkerchief" (73). While both parents warn their children not to spend the money (essentially denying its function as money), Lincoln's money is not "rolled up and tied up tight" but only "in a clean handkerchief." Even the father's way of warning Lincoln not to spend the money is highly ironic: the cash is in a handkerchief, and he asks the boy not to "go blowing it" (a phrase that continues the play's association of money with bodily emissions) (73).

Lincoln not only spends money but also, in an important sense, *is* money. A recurring motif in the play associates Lincoln with the $5 bill (the American paper currency denomination that bears the image of President Lincoln) or at least with the number five. After divvying up Lincoln's pay (in his own favor), Booth asks Lincoln for a "5-spot" (41). Earlier, Lincoln tells how, dressed as the President, he asked a child on the bus for $10 in exchange for the autograph the boy asks for, and explains "I was gonna say 5, cause of the Lincoln connection" (15). During a practice game of monte Lincoln asks Booth to "slap" him "5" (82). Booth once refers to Lincoln in his Abe Lincoln costume as dressed up "like some dead president," "dead president" being a well-known term in American hip-hop culture for money (27).[15]

A closer look at the character of Lincoln shows he represents several of the qualities typically associated with money. Lincoln is the uncanny embodiment of money's tendency to complicate the relation of appearance to reality, the symbolic to the real. Always and everywhere in this play, Lincoln's words, actions, and mere appearance foreground the discrepancies between surface and meaning, nature and mimesis, intellectual and material value that so traumatize his younger brother Booth.

To look at the issue of "essential" vs. "surface" identity as embodied in Lincoln is to experience the vertigo of stripping away layer upon seemingly endless layer of meaning. On the surface Lincoln is dressed like the nation's sixteenth President, which includes (in addition to the familiar coat, stovepipe hat, and beard) whiteface make-up. The role Lincoln plays at his job also bleeds into his life outside work, as we learn when he tells Booth that on his way home from work, a child on the bus asked him for his autograph (15). "Underneath" this outward layer is a man trying to escape his past (as a three-card-monte hustler), an act his brother Booth tries to convince him is untrue to who he *really is.* Then of course, "Lincoln" happens to be the character's "real" name, but one, his father tells him, which was given him as "a joke" (29). Even on a purely literary level, Lincoln simultaneously opens and closes a space between the authentic and the mimetic: he is preceded by another character who portrays Abraham Lincoln for a living in Parks's *The America Play,* though the playwright insists Lincoln (of *Topdog/Underdog)* is "unrelated to the first guy" ("Introduction" 4). In the character of Lincoln, Parks sets up a situation in which simple distinctions between depth and surface, reality and performance refuse to hold.

Lincoln similarly problematizes distinctions between two ways of thinking about identity and about race: as "essential" or as "performed." Dressed as the President and wearing whiteface, Lincoln is an uncanny reminder of the performativity of identity. At the same time, the Abe Lincoln "get-up" makes us (and apparently would make Lincoln) intensely aware of Lincoln's (and the actor's) "blackness." The very effectiveness of Lincoln onstage dressed as Abe Lincoln relies on his blackness as an "essential" quality, even as it highlights the performativity of "race." In an essay she calls "Elements of Style," Parks uses the following example to illustrate her belief that "content determines form and form determines content; that form and content are interdependent": "I am an African American woman – this is the form I take, my content predicates this form, and this form is inseparable from my content. No way could I be me otherwise" (7, 8). Parks's statement shows her resisting the naturalist logic that recognizes everything as ontologically *either* content or form, nature or mimesis. Through her own chosen example and through the character of Lincoln in *Topdog/Underdog,* Parks demonstrates how this narrow naturalist logic has limited the ways we may think about who we are.

Clothing again becomes an important symbol of the paradoxical idea of identity Lincoln embodies. When Lincoln tries on a suit that Booth has stolen for him, the younger brother (unsurprisingly, given that character's notion that controlling signs allows one to control the real) tells Lincoln that the suit makes him "look like the real you" (34). For Booth, this "real" Lincoln that reappears via the stolen suit is the one who looks like Lincoln "used to look" before he stopped hustling and took a legitimate job (34). Lincoln's ideas about clothes and identity, however, are more complicated. Although "[t]hey say the clothes make the man," he tells

Booth, "[a]ll day long I wear that getup. But that dont make me who I am" (33). Here Lincoln tries to clearly differentiate between his "real" identity and the one he takes on to earn a living. His position is a direct challenge to the one apparently espoused by his brother: that clothes *do* make him who he is, that signs fully determine the real. Lincoln similarly corrects Booth, whose statements repeatedly seem to confuse Lincoln with the role he plays. "He shoot you?" Booth asks of one of Lincoln's "customers." Lincoln responds, "He shot Honest Abe, yeah" (38). Yet at other moments Lincoln's statements and actions regarding clothing seem to indicate doubt as to the seemingly hard line he would draw between surface and reality. We learn, for instance, that after his father left him and Booth, Lincoln burned his father's clothes. He tells Booth that he "got tired of looking at em without him in em," but the need to utterly destroy the clothes is at odds with his statements downgrading the importance of clothes to the making of identity (33). The importance of clothes – or the inextricable link between surface and "essential" identity – is also revealed in Lincoln's disturbed reaction to waking up in his "getup" in Scene Four. Before Lincoln states that he "[h]ate[s] falling asleep in this damn shit," Parks's stage directions tell us Lincoln *"claws at his Lincoln getup, removing it and tearing it in the process"* (59). Despite Lincoln's professed attitude when he first took this unusual job–"I would make a living at it," he says, "[b]ut it dont make me" (34) – he is clearly ill at ease regarding the difficulty of drawing a line between who he is and who he appears to be, and a confusion between his role and his "real" self repeatedly breaks through to the surface. Lincoln's perspective on the relation of performance to identity becomes more complicated as the play progresses, until at one point he refers to the "[d]ust from the cap guns on the left shoulder where they shoot him, where they shoot me I should say but I never feel like they shooting me" (33).

This tangle of self and role is stated in brilliantly uncanny fashion in the words of a mysterious man Lincoln refers to as his "Best Customer" (38). This man accompanies his simulated shooting of Lincoln with statements like the following: "Does thuh show stop when no ones watching or does thuh show go on?" and "Yr only yrself [. . .] when no ones watching" (39). The Best Customer is himself of murky identity: Lincoln says he "think[s]" the man is "a brother" but can't be sure; nor can he tell if the man knows that Lincoln is black. Booth, with unconscious irony, comments that the Best Customer is "a *deep* black brother" – this about a figure who taunts Lincoln with the notion that all is surface, or that the distinction between depth and surface is ultimately an elusive one (39). The first statement of this avatar of the brothers' deepest anxieties questions the very existence of an "essential" self that does not involve some kind of performance. The second statement opens the door just a crack for the possibility of an essential self, but limits its existence to very rare moments: in the world of the play as in modern American life, someone is almost always "watching." In fact the "patter" Lincoln rattles off as he throws the cards in the confidence game of three-card monte includes the much-repeated phrase "watch me": "One good pickll get you in, 2 good picks and you gone win. Watch me come on watch me now" (62). The extent to which Lincoln has internalized a view of himself as something to be displayed may inform how he announces his own entrance (repeatedly) with a familiar magician's phrase for presenting the key effect of a trick: "Taaaaadaaaaaaaa!" (30, 86).

The enigmatic statements of the Best Customer, the paradoxical role of clothing (and, more specifically, of costume) as both concealer and creator of identity, the arbitrarily given yet ominously portentous historical names of the characters, and Lincoln's unusual job all no doubt create a highly metatheatrical experience for an audience watching *Topdog/Underdog* performed on a stage. We may add to this list two additional metatheatrical elements that more explicitly tie the play's complicating of the distinction between surface and depth to money. The first of these elements is that of the family.

We are presented in the play with two brothers who are, in a sense, play-acting the traditional, nuclear-family roles of mother and father, each brother's role coinciding with the role of the parent who paid him his "inheritance." Booth, who received his money from his mother, acts what has been until recently the traditional role of the woman in the American nuclear family: he does not earn money; he chooses clothes for both himself and Link; he even redecorates the apartment at one point, turning the crates he uses to practice monte into a table setting with *"two nice chairs," "a lovely tablecloth,"* and *"nice plates, silverware, champagne glasses and candles,"* as well as hanging new curtains and even placing *"a doily-like object on the recliner"* in anticipation of Grace's arrival (which of course never happens) (62-3). Lincoln, who received his $500 from his father, plays the traditional role of the husband and father: he leaves the house to work every day and spends his time in the apartment on a recliner – that great symbol of American masculine domestic leisure. These roles seem to be adopted by the brothers largely unconsciously; however, in the second scene of the play, the two engage in a very self-conscious, highly metatheatrical performance in which they play-act a minstrel-show stereotype of a black family, even calling themselves "Ma" and "Pa" (30). Significantly, this scene centers on Lincoln's bringing home his week's pay. "Lordamighty, Pa, I smells money!" exclaims Booth as his brother enters. Answers Lincoln, "Sho nuff, Ma. Poppa done brung home thuh bacon" (30). The self-conscious minstrelsy continues as Lincoln brings the money to Booth with *"a series of very elaborate moves"* (30). Finally, Booth asks Lincoln to "[p]ut it in my hands." Lincoln insists "I want ya tuh smells it first, Ma!" and "Take yrself a good long whiff of them greenbacks" (30). This highly ironic scene is crucial to understanding the symbolic role of money in the play. In their play-acting, Lincoln and Booth celebrate not the spending power of money – not the possibilities that having this money opens up – but the money as *physical substance.* Of course, to emphasize this concrete, physical dimension of money is to emphasize what is at odds with the very nature of money, which is always undergoing what Simmel calls a continual process of "spiritualization" (Poggi 161). By fetishizing the money *as an object* available to the senses, the brothers transform – if only for a moment – those threatening "greenbacks" (they even use that antiquated and physicalizing term from the gold-standard debates) into a concrete substance, reversing money's trend toward the immaterial, *naturalizing* the money if you will, denying its threatening unreality. We should also remember that the boys' real family life was essentially replaced by money when the mother and father paid each brother and left. This fantasy of a return to the traditional American family then necessitates the repression of money. This transformation of money from symbol into the "real" is accomplished, significantly, through a minstrel-show performance that complicates the notion of Lincoln's and Booth's "blackness" as either *real* or *unreal* / performative. Michael Germana notes how minstrel performances in antebellum America were "preoccupied with the slippage between inherent value and face value," as the performers (typically white Northerners "blacked up" with burnt cork) simultaneously encoded "race" as both essential and performative (21).

Parks's investigations into the idea of authentic blackness and the idea of "real" money may remind one of the now-popular hip-hop colloquialism, "keeping it real." The phrase often implies that its speaker is maintaining an authentic black self by avoiding a certain kind of economic "success" – by not "selling out." The phrase's connection between the idea of authenticity (or the "real") and the realm of economics, and the place of race in this relation, is explored in a similar way in a television sketch from comedian Dave Chappelle's controversial, critically acclaimed *Chappelle Show*. During its second season, just two years after *Topdog/Underdog* debuted on Broadway, Chappelle's show began a series of sketches called "When Keeping It Real Goes Wrong." The first sketch of this series features a character named Vernon Franklin, whom a voice-over tells us is an "exceptional" black success story: class valedictorian, first in his family to attend college, and now the youngest vice-president of a major corporation, "ending the cycle of violence and drug addiction that had plagued his family for generations." Vernon is shown making some sort of presentation to a boardroom full of white "corporate types." When Vernon finishes his presentation, a white businessman who we are told is his "mentor" turns to him and exclaims "You the man!" and "Gimme some skin!" The camera momentarily freezes so as to underscore the importance of this moment for the future of the sketch's protagonist. During the freeze-frame, the voice-over tells us that "Vernon got along with all of the people he worked with, which in his heart of hearts, made him feel like an Uncle Tom. Though he could have ignored the simple comment his mentor made, Vernon decided to 'keep it real.'" When the frame unfreezes, Chappelle's character responds to his white colleague's minstrelsy with explosive anger: "Get your motherfuckin' hand out of my face." He asks why the white man cannot simply "shake [his] hand like a man," then asks if he'd like to see any other bits of minstrelsy while he's at it: "You want a little soft shoe? Should I jump watermelons?" The skit concludes with a glimpse of Chappelle's character at some time after this encounter. The formerly well-dressed and economically successful businessman now works at "Sunny's Fill-Er-Up on route eighty in New Jersey" and makes "$6.45 an hour." Now, the voice-over tells us, "It's as real as it can be." Finally, we witness Vernon reject a $1 tip with the words, "What am I gonna get with a dollar nigger, I got kids! And that's *real!*" Vernon throws down his squeegee and walks away, as if to quit his job. The voice-over ends the skit this way: "Vernon Franklin: once a heartwarming story of perseverance, today a startling example of when 'keeping it real' goes wrong."

By asking him to "give" him "some skin," Chappelle's character's white "mentor" is in essence asking him to perform that white character's conception of blackness. Such a performance would, by the logic of the sketch, receive a significant financial and social payoff. By choosing instead to be "real," by refusing to be the black man the white man wants him to be, Chappelle's character disrupts the performance of racial harmony that the uniformly dressed businessmen would enact. That this harmony is in fact a performance is demonstrated by the very request of the white businessman, which shows that he is always aware of his black colleague's "difference." By asking his colleague to slap him five, the white businessman enters into a performance of blackness that in turn demands a performance from the black man – that is, it demands that the black man perform his own blackness; it demands nothing less (or more) than that he experience that alienated self Dubois called "double-consciousness." Disrupting this performance, demanding an authentic if contentious relation to his racist white colleagues – keeping it "real" – brings the black businessman an enormous financial and social cost. At the same time, the sketch seems to undermine any distinction between the "before" and "after" of the black businessman's decision, for if he consented to the performance for which he was being asked by his white colleague, he would in a sense now also be playing the supplicant, but a better-paid one. Chappelle's sketch thus problematizes the deceptively simple critical axiom that "identity is performed" by pointing out the very different existential *and* economic stakes of two performances: a white businessman performing a black "other," and a black businessman compelled to perform his own blackness, making himself the other. At the same time, the sketch suggests that contemporary African American conceptions of authenticity need to be rethought – it calls for a more nuanced conception of "keeping it real." The black character's keeping it "real" by quitting his job at the gas station at the end of the skit shows the serious implications of this idea, as an insistence that an "authentic" blackness cannot coexist with economic success leads to a downward social spiral.

It is of course more than coincidental that the period in America that saw the flourishing of the minstrelsy both Parks and Chappelle are investigating was also the period of the most heightened anxieties regarding money and its apparently arbitrary relation to what the metallists thought of as a "natural value." The figuring of blackness around the semantic axis of authentic essence *or* "necessary fiction" (or performance) partakes of the logic of naturalism Benn Michaels traces to the American gold-standard debates, with their pitched rhetorical battles between the "hard-money" advocates and those favoring the "greenback." By this logic, money is either a sign of the artificiality of a black selfhood, or a sign of a black selfhood created by an act of (white) Congressmen. We see in these nineteenth-century arguments the seeds of the choice Parks's and Chappelle's characters are forced to make at the dawn of the twenty-first century: between an inessential blackness symbolized by money, and an essential blackness threatened by money; put differently, the choice is between an economically rewarding alienation and an economically impoverished authenticity.

A final metatheatrical element of *Topdog/Underdog* explicitly associated with the brothers' fear/repression of money is the confidence game of three-card monte that is at the very heart of the play. The "game" itself, like virtually all confidence games, is highly theatrical, combining carefully orchestrated speech and movement designed to create a specific effect in the audience. The monte dealer is part of a "crew" that includes the "Sideman" (who pretends to play and win, thus luring unsuspecting marks to the game), a "Stickman" (here, an unspecified role with violent implications) and a "Lookout" (76). As Lincoln repeatedly (and unsuccessfully) tries to teach Booth, the various elements of the hustle – the talk (the "patter"), the moves, the eye contact – are *all* essential parts of the game. The game's great lesson is, ironically, just what Booth fears: the difficulty of reading signs, and the impossibility of the "mark's" discerning, in Lincoln's words, "what is" from "what aint" (77).

The great irony of Booth's desperation to acquire his brother's skill as a three-card monte master is that despite the street-tough attitude of his speech and actions, Booth persists in a kind of relentless idealism when it comes to the game. As Lincoln well knows, a good monte dealer *never* loses money to a customer: the dealer allows the player to gain a false confidence by winning a couple of rounds for small or no stakes, then fleeces him. The game, of course, is crooked. Yet Booth believes the player has a fair chance of winning, seeing the winning of the game as a combination of skill and luck: "Sure thered be some cats out there with fast eyes, some brothers and sisters who would watch real close and pick the right card, and so thered be some days when we would lose money," he tells his brother (24). Just a moment later, when Lincoln argues that his current job playing Abe Lincoln is not a "hustle" because his customers "know the real deal," Booth argues, "We do the card game people will know the real deal. Sometimes we will win sometimes they will win. They fast they win, we faster we win" (27). A little while later Booth says Lincoln "was lucky with the cards," and Lincoln again tries to show him the truth: "Cards aint luck. Cards is skill. Aint never nothing lucky about the cards" (40).

A more powerful instance of Booth's failure to see the essential nature of the game of monte occurs in Scene Five. When Booth refers to the monte dealer's "customer," Lincoln sees an opportunity to correct his younger brother's misperception: "Thuh customer," he tells him, "is actually called the 'Mark,'" then asks, "You know why?" Booth answers, "Cause hes thuh one you got yr eye on. You mark him with yr eye" (75). Booth utterly fails to see the violent implications in the terminology of the game, "mark" meaning not just that the player is marked by the dealer's eye, but that he is a target. Along with older definitions of "mark" including "the quarry of a hawk," the Oxford English Dictionary lists meanings very close to Lincoln's: "[a]mong criminals: a person, property, etc., targeted for robbery or burglary; (also) an item to be stolen"; and "[a] person who is easily persuaded, deceived, or taken advantage of; a victim targeted by a swindler, cheat, etc."

Booth's naiveté about the game of monte is of a piece with his refusal to recognize any distinction between "business" relationships and "family" relationships – a trait that is, ironically, both the cause of Booth's tragedy and the only thing that he thinks may save him. Booth's desperate plans to "team up" with Lincoln are of course thinly veiled attempts to re-establish some kind of *intimate* connection with his brother. When, in the first scene, Booth proposes that he become Lincoln's "Stickman," Booth says he'd be "The one in the crowd who looks just like an innocent passerby, who looks just like another player, like just another customer, but who gots intimate connections with you" (24). These lines capture Booth's fear of the distanced, alienated world of economic exchange and his desperate need to replace that with intimacy: he does not want to be "just another customer" but to have "intimate connections" with his brother (to whom he now refers not as "Lincoln" but, tellingly, as "link" –i.e. the link he needs to form with another human being) (24). Working the con with Lincoln is the only way Booth knows to try to re-establish the familial bond that was shattered when his parents left. "I didnt mind them leaving," says Booth, "cause you was there. Thats why Im hooked on us working together. If we could work together it would be like old times. [. . .] It was you and me against thuh world, Link. It could be like that again" (74). The extent of Booth's Loman-esque entangling of love with economic life may be measured by his apparent belief that his parents' paying him and his brother $500 each and abandoning them was an act of romantic love – evidence, reasons Booth, that the couple "had some agreement between them": "Somewhere in there when it looked like all they had was hate they sat down and did thuh 'split' budget," Booth reasons. "Theyd been scheming together all along. They left separately but they was in agreement. Maybe they arrived at the same time, maybe they renewed their wedding vows, maybe they got another family" (73).

If, in regard to the entangling of economic relationships with family relationships, Booth plays the naïf, Lincoln assumes the role of disillusioning teacher. In Scene Five, during one of his attempts to teach Booth what he is not capable of learning about the life of the confidence artist, Lincoln stares at Booth in a manner that seems to unnerve his younger brother. The older brother explains, "Im sizing you up" (77). Booth's explosion only demonstrates his naïveté: "Oh yeah?! [. . .] "Im on yr Side, Link, Im on yr team, you dont go sizing up yr own team. You save looks like that for yr Mark" (77). Lincoln is of course trying to teach

Booth the existential price paid by the confidence artist, and perhaps by us all, in a money economy: that, in this way of life, everyone is a potential "mark," and there is no "team" in the way Booth uses that term. "Dealer always sizes up the crowd," explains Lincoln. "Everybody out there is part of the crowd. His crew is part of the crowd, he himself is part of the crowd. Dealer always sizes up thuh crowd" (78). The level of alienation and distrust of *all* other people – and alienation and distrust even of *himself* ("he himself," says Lincoln, "is part of the crowd" to be sized up) is precisely what terrifies the younger Booth.[16] Thus does Lincoln put his own disillusioning spin on Booth's romantic notion of their parents' escaping together: "Maybe they got 2 new kids," posits Lincoln. "2 boys. Different than us, though. Better" (73-4). Lincoln's brief statement replaces Booth's romantic fantasy with another vision, one in which money (in the form of those $500 "inheritance[s]") symbolizes the complete loss of the boys' individuality, their reduction to an easily replaceable commodity: if the parents don't like them, they can simply pay them off and find two "better" boys.

The apparent attitudes of Lincoln and Booth toward the game of three-card monte – Booth's desperately idealistic vision and Lincoln's disillusioned, "realist" one – are part of what emerges in the play as a complex meditation on the nature of the real. Unsurprisingly Lincoln, that uncanny manifestation of money and its seeming ability to make the real unreal and the unreal real, is at the heart of this meditation. While Lincoln has in one sense given up the life of the confidence man, his "legitimate" occupation as a pretend Abraham Lincoln is, as Booth tells him, still a kind of "hustle," though Lincoln insists on the distinction that his current customers "know the real deal" – that is, the customers know that this is all make-believe. "When people know the real deal," insists Lincoln, "it aint a hustle" (26-7). Yet the words of the mysterious man Lincoln calls his "Best Customer" undermine Lincoln's tidy distinction: "Does thuh show stop when no ones watching or does thuh show go on?" and "Yr only yrself [. .] when no ones watching" (38, 39). And when Lincoln tells Booth that there has been talk at the arcade of replacing him with a wax figure (unsurprising since Lincoln, as money incarnate, represents money's tendency to reduce all to a least common denominator, to make all ultimately replaceable), the younger brother suggests Lincoln "jazz up" his "act" by making his death scenes at the arcade more *realistic* (40). In Scene Three Parks stages another highly metatheatrical episode where Booth repeatedly pretends to shoot Lincoln and the older brother holds his head, moans, and generally goes (as the stage directions tell us) *"all out"* (56-7). The result is that Lincoln's acting makes the scene look "too real"

– an unacceptable result, as Lincoln explains:

> They don't want it looking too real. I'd scare the customers. [. . . .] People are funny about they Lincoln shit. Its historical. People like they historical shit in a certain way. They like it to unfold the way they folded it up. Neatly like a book. Not raggedy and bloody and screaming. (57)

The lines contradict Lincoln's earlier statement that his current customers know the "real deal"; they are certainly, it seems, fooling themselves with Lincoln's help, transforming the "raggedy and bloody and screaming" reality of history into a clean, bloodless affair.

While the arcade where Lincoln works obscures one kind of reality by giving people their history the way they'd prefer to see it, Lincoln, in his role as the President, does feel he gains momentary access to the real in an interesting way. At his job, he explains, he is not able to look directly at the people who shoot him, since he is "supposed to be staring straight ahead. Watching a play, like Abe was" (53-4). The "assassins," whom Lincoln describes as groups of schoolchildren, businessmen, "[t]ourists in they theme park t-shirts trying to catch it all on film," and "[h]ousewives with they mouths closed tight, shooting more than once," walk up behind Lincoln and "shoot" him from a spot marked on the carpet (54-5). While his back is to his shooter, Lincoln explains that he can see the shooter's upside-down reflection in a dented metal fusebox. He describes the encounter:

> And when the gun touches me he can feel that Im warm and he knows Im alive. And if Im alive then he can shoot me dead. And for a minute, with him hanging back there behind me, its real. Me looking at him upside down and him looking at me looking like Lincoln. Then he shoots. (54)

Here, any simple distinction between real and unreal is problematized. The encounter is in one sense marked by several levels of artificiality. First, all of this is of course happening on a stage before an audience. Within the play, Lincoln is of course playing the role of President Lincoln. The schoolchildren are costumed in their "uniforms." The tourists' "theme park t-shirts" and their attempts to "catch it all on film" further denote the artificiality of their encounter (54-5). Yet in the midst of this highly artificial, highly mediated encounter, the upside-down reflection of the dented fusebox seems to play a kind of defamiliarizing role that permits the participants access to reality, if only for a moment.

It is perhaps not insignificant that Lincoln describes the reflective box that gives him access to the real as "Silver metal" (54). The logic of naturalism (a logic born of the fear and repression of money) is one that divides the world into two categories: those things that are, simply and essentially, "real," and those things that pretend to be something else entirely. Gold and silver are "real," the paper money that would become these precious metals' equivalent is deceptively imitative. The aesthetic analog to this logic is a view that sees all aesthetic objects as *either* natural beauty *or* "mimesis." A sunset is (according to this logic) either just a sunset or, in the familiar phrase, "pretty as a postcard": "It is as if we can love the sunset either as a sunset or as the representation of a painting," but not as both simultaneously (Benn Michaels157). What this logic is incapable of conceiving is that, just as the mimetic properties of gold are an essential part of its "reality" (and its assumed reality an essential part of its mimetic role), "natural" beauty and mimesis are deeply involved in one another. In his analysis of Norris's novel *McTeague,* Benn Michaels notes that the miser (and junk-shop owner) Zerkow transcends this logic when he loves Maria's stories about her lost gold tea service (mimetic representations of gold) as much as he loves gold itself. Here the "distinction between his desire for gold and his desire for the description gets lost" because "the representation is here understood to be an essential part of the gold itself":

> If Zerkow's fancy is a mirror that reflects the gold, and if Maria's language is a mirror that reproduces it in simile, then the gold itself is also a mirror, so that in taking the representation for the thing itself, Zerkow is not making some quixotic mistake about fictions and the real but is instead rightly recognizing the representation as an ontological piece of the thing. (Benn Michaels 158-9)

In *Topdog/Underdog,* Lincoln's meditation on the highly artificial, theme-park encounter with his make-believe "assassin" becoming momentarily "real" as the event is reflected in the "Silver metal" of the dented fusebox is, like Zerkow's refusal to distinguish between actual gold and stories about gold, not evidence of the character's failure to distinguish real from imitation, but rather evidence of the imitative's inextricable link to the real, and vice versa. Escaping the narrow logic of naturalism, Lincoln's experience is both mimetic and real.

Parks's placing the character of Lincoln – that "dead president" or money embodied – at the center of this scene involving the dialectical relation of reality and mimesis thematically associates that dialectic with money. As the play reaches its climax, that association is deepened through Booth's final lessons in the confidence game of three-card monte. As a good confidence artist would, Lincoln apparently allows Booth to win two rounds of the game. The younger brother still of course does not understand the fundamentally misleading character of the game, and struts around after each success. Then something about the game bothers him: "You gotta do it for real, man" he tells his brother. "It didnt feel real" (101). Lincoln, who understands the game as a type of theatre (and understands that the seemingly superficial or theatrical elements of the game are simultaneously irreplaceable parts of the game's "reality") explains that several of the "essential elements" –"[t]he crowd, the street, thuh traffic sounds, all that" – are "missing," but Booth is focused on what is, to his mind, the one element that can make the game "real": "We missing something else too, thuh thing thatll really make it real [. . .] Thuh cash. Its just bullshit without thuh money. Put some money down on thuh table then itd be real, then youd do it for real, then I'd win it for real" (101). Lincoln obliges: "I put my money down," he says; "[m]oney makes it real" (103). Booth, obliged now to match Lincoln's $500 bet, puts down that nylon stocking containing (he assumes) $500: his "inheritance." "Now its real," he declares, having placed his bet (105). Of course, in the third round of the game, Lincoln wins Booth's money.

In these last moments of the play, money takes on the full complement of its complex associations. Remember that Booth repeatedly demonstrates a preference for symbols over reality. Just as Willy Loman prefers the idea of his son Biff (or the romantic memory of Biff) to the actual, concrete Biff, Booth exists inside the relative safety of imagined sex, the lies he tells himself about Grace's love, and his grandiose plans for the future – he is always "scheming and dreaming," to use a phrase repeatedly associated with Booth throughout the play (92). The money wrapped in his mother's nylon stocking is a powerful symbol of Booth's preference for symbol over the real: not only hasn't he spent this money, but he has never even untied the stocking to verify the money's existence. As long as the package remains unopened, Booth can believe what he wants to believe. As Lincoln says, not realizing that this is exactly why Booth never untied the stocking, "There could be millions in here! There could be nothing!" (110).

Lincoln, as the incarnation of money in this play, relentlessly taunts Booth with doubts concerning the reality Booth desperately needs to believe in but suspects does not exist. Lincoln wonders aloud if he and Booth are even brothers; Booth answers "I think we're brothers" (107). Lincoln says of their mother, "she handed you this stocking and she said there was money in it and then she split and you say you didn't open it. Howd you know she was for real?" (110). Booth simply answers "She was for real," but Lincoln persists in disillusioning his younger brother, culminating in his final lesson on the game of monte: it's "thuh first move," he tells Booth, "that separates thuh Player from thuh Played":

> And thuh first move is to know that there aint no winning. [. . .] It may look like you got a chance but the only time you pick right is when thuh man lets you. And when its thuh real deal, when its the real fucking deal, bro, and thuh moneys on the line, thats when thuh man wont want you picking right. He will want you picking wrong so he will make you pick wrong. (111)

Booth wanted to make things "real" by playing for money, but the real is exactly what he most fears. So we may not be surprised to learn, in the closing moments of the play, that Booth has killed Grace, thus removing the possibility of replacing his symbolic sex life with an actual one. Grace apparently paid with her life for trying to force Booth to face reality: "Who the fuck she think she is," asks Booth, "[t]elling me I don't got nothing going on" (112). Lincoln's threatening to cut open the nylon stocking to expose the reality (the existence or the non-existence) of Booth's "inheritance" is similarly something Booth cannot let happen. "We *know* whats in it," insists Booth, "Don't open it" (110). When Lincoln learns that Booth has shot and killed Grace, the older brother seems to grasp the extent of Booth's fear of the actual and reverses course, trying to give the stocking back to Booth. Now it is Booth who orders Lincoln to "OPEN IT!!!" (113). As Lincoln brings the knife down, Booth shoots and kills him. Now Booth can remain inside the imaginary world he has created. He is, he announces, now no longer Booth but "3 Card," a name he insists will "be in everybodys head and in everybodys mouth like Link was" (114). Booth's intense need to control symbols (and thus, he thinks, control the real) ultimately leaves him alone in his own hell: a small room where nothing enters or exits – what Una Chaudhuri describes as "a room with a vengeance" (289).

Parks has written about what she calls "the special strange relationship between theatre and real-life" ("Possession" 4). Since a play is not simply a text but a specific event that, as Parks writes, *"actually happens,"* each of her plays functions as "an incubator to create 'new' historical events." "I'm re-membering and staging historical events which," writes Parks, "through their happening on stage, are ripe for inclusion in the canon of history. Theatre is an incubator for the creation of historical events – and, as in the case of artificial insemination, the baby is no less human" (4-5). Katy Ryan correctly points out that this statement implies "an understanding that history is always mediated knowledge" (83). Haike Frank adds that Parks's view of theatre as "actually happen[ing]" "seem[s] to suggest that reality is based on subjective representation and that an objective version of reality, including historical reality, can only be achieved by a multiplicity of perspectives" (5). The (deceptively) simple distinction between the real and the mimetic that is the obsession of naturalism is thus undermined by Parks's dramaturgy. As Parks complicates a simple distinction between the real and the mimetic, so does she explode the dichotomy of text/performance. As W.B. Worthen points out, Parks's plays tend to be at once self-consciously performative in their use of repetition and metatheatre, and highly textual in their focus on the "mediating role of print in our understanding of history" (4-5). Unlike a playwright like Mamet who, despite his plays' forays into the postmodern, insists on the written text's ability to contain the author's "meaning," Parks recognizes a more complicated relationship between text and performance, where each is intimately involved in the creation of the other.

The complex model of perception that is ultimately endorsed by the play finds its metaphor in the game of monte as described by Lincoln. As he tries to teach Booth, the truth lies not in words alone (the "patter"), nor in the lightening-fast movements of the dealer. Word and body, "talk" and action, are both necessary, as are what Lincoln refers to as the other "essential elements" –"[t]he crowd, the street, thuh traffic sounds, all that" (103). This is ultimately a highly theatrical model of perception, and one that clearly informs Suzan-Lori Parks's stagecraft. In *Topdog/Underdog,* as in other plays she has written, Parks employs what she calls her own "slightly unconventional theatrical elements" ("Author's Note" 5). The first she calls a *"(Rest)"* and represents a place where the actor should "Take a little time, a pause, a breather; make a transition." The second and more significant one for our focus here Parks calls a "Spell." Denoted in the text by the character's name in all capital letters with no dialogue attached, Parks describes the Spell as "a place where the characters experience their pure true simple state." "While no action or stage business is necessary," explains Parks, "directors should fill this moment as they best see fit." Parks writes that the "feeling" of a Spell is that of a daguerreotype, or the "music of [the] spheres." A Spell is "a place of great (unspoken) emotion," and also "a place for an emotional transition" ("From 'Elements of Style'"16-17). At first glance Parks's apparently essentialist notion of a character's "pure true simple state" seems itself to be an instance of the fear/repression of language at the heart of naturalism. But Parks only employs the Spell as one element among others, including (of course) the word. As Jennifer Johung points out in her discussion of this device in the excerpt "Scene of Love(?)" from Parks's play *Venus,* the Spell is also another way Parks explodes a simple distinction between text and performance: it "necessitates an adjustment in the way that readers and producers of Parks's work think about the intersections between the activities of writing and performing, as well as the interactions between the interpretation of the written marks on the page and the embodiment of the corporeal markings of performers onstage" (41). Thus does Parks demonstrate how the drama is uniquely placed to escape the narrow logic of naturalism. In theatre, the written text of the play is of course only one part of the play's totality. Writers like Parks who consciously employ the actors' and the director's non-verbal contributions to the creation of character and of drama on stage go perhaps further than the writer of fiction may possibly go in creating works that explore the dialectical relation of material to identity, action to talk, material value to face value – a dialectic embodied in money.

At the same time, *Topdog/Underdog* ultimately raises more questions than it answers in regard to the complicated issue of identity as performative, and the role of money in that performance. The older brother Lincoln may have a more complicated understanding of the relation of signs to the real, and an appreciation of the way the "representation" is an "ontological piece of the thing." Nevertheless, he is able to save neither his brother nor himself. If money's role in helping to create that which it only seems to represent is emphasized in the "reality" Lincoln briefly glimpses in a piece of silver during his performance, it must be remembered that the performance in question is one of which he is ultimately not in control, but does only out of a need for money. Moreover, the money that Lincoln seems to gain power by spending ultimately proves to be beyond his power to control as well, and at play's end his brother Booth is left with money, his new (performed) identity, and nothing else.

***

Suzan-Lori Parks's play *In The Blood* premiered at the Papp Public Theater in New York in November 1999, directed by David Esbjornson. Critics familiar with Parks's oeuvre saw the play as somewhat of a departure from her earlier work in its move toward realism, or at the very least in its interesting blend of realism and self-conscious theatricality. Vincent Canby, for instance, noted that the world of the play is "exotic" but "never for a moment does it seem to be unreal or removed," and David Krasner pointed out that while the play does make use of "nonrealistic devices," it differs from earlier plays by Parks in its use of "realistic settings and psychological characterizations" (Canby 7, Krasner 565).

Fucking A opened in February 2000 at Diverse Works/Infernal Bridegroom Productions in Houston, in a production directed by Parks in collaboration with the company. The play was later produced at the Papp Public Theater as well (in March 2003), directed by Michael Greif. While critical response to *Fucking A* was generally less positive than it was for Parks's previous play (John Simon and Charles Isherwood found the tragic ending unconvincing, and both Simon and Ben Brantley found the play's use of Brechtian dramaturgy unimaginatively derivative), most reviews noted the play's mixture or Brechtian and realistic theatrical devices. Brantley for instance saw the play as mixing "Brechtian distance with the kind of intense social melodrama associated with Clifford Odets."

While generally produced separately, the two plays have come to be grouped by critics as Parks's "Red Letter Plays" – so named because in both plays, Parks, by her own description, "riffs" on Hawthorne's classic American novel *The Scarlet Letter.* Like Hawthorne's novel, Park's two plays both feature protagonists named Hester. In *In The Blood,* Hester La Negrita, an illiterate and destitute mother of five, interacts with various characters representing institutional forces of American society that while ostensibly meant to help her, instead collude in her exploitation. In *Fucking A*, Hester Smith, an illiterate abortionist, is driven by an intense desire for revenge on a rich woman whose "snitching" sent her son to prison. Both plays end with the protagonist killing her own son, and while there are important contextual differences between the two killings, in each case this final act ironically underscores a tragic lack of agency on the part of the heroine. At the end of both plays, neither the heroine's own situation nor the social structures with which she clashes has changed significantly.

A less obvious but, in the view of this study, a crucial similarity between the Red Letter plays and Hawthorne's novel is the two works' interrogation of American attitudes toward the relation of the symbolic to the real. As an external visual marker of what is supposed by other characters as its wearer's "internal," "spiritual" state, Hester Prynne's Scarlet "A" is, among other things, an emblem of a powerful American anxiety regarding the gulf between appearance and reality. The desperate and dangerous need for fixed signs and self-evident identities that obsesses Hawthorne's characters likewise informs *In The Blood* and *Fucking A,* and Parks's plays locate the root of this attitude in economic life.

While critics almost universally acknowledge Parks's concern with the economic structures of society, and while several critics investigate Parks's obsession with the verbal and visual sign and its relation to racial, cultural, and gender identities, very little work has been done to investigate the connection between these two aspects of her work.[17] Over the past four decades the work of "New Economic" critics has read money as a symbol of a troubling discrepancy between the symbolic and the real, or what Shell calls "material" and "intellectual currency" (1). An anxiety over this discrepancy informs Parks's work generally, but it finds its fullest exploration in the Red Letter plays[18]. Very early in *In the Blood,* a chorus of characters observe of the "welfare queen" Hester, La Negrita, "BAD NEWS IN HER BLOOD/ PLAIN AS DAY"(7). In a similar vein, in *Fucking A,* protagonist Hester Smith would overcome the ambiguity of appearances by physically marking her son so as to always be able to recognize him. Nevertheless, the repeated and deeply tragic failures at recognition that characterize both plays undercut their characters' insistence on reliable verbal and visual signs, and in both plays money and economic thinking is shown to be inextricably bound up with this dilemma.

A need for money drives the plots of both plays: *In the Blood's* Hester tries and fails to gain financial support from the fathers of her five "treasures"; *Fucking A's* Hester tries and fails to earn enough money to buy her imprisoned son's freedom. More significantly, each play gives us a world in which relations between characters are transformed in disturbing ways by money. In *In The Blood*, a preacher named Reverend D runs a "salvation business," a welfare worker says she cares about people because she is paid to, an expectant mother plans to sell the valuable "fruit of [her] white womb" *(In the Blood* 55, 71). In the second play, the "kept woman" Canary's lover "owns [her] exclusive rights," and unwanted pregnancies are good for the economy: "Their troubles yr livelihood," explains the abortionist Hester Smith to herself (117). In the worlds of these two plays, human life on every level has been transformed into an abstraction by the reification of money and economic relations.

By focusing on the related examples of the too sexually prolific "Welfare Queen" and the abortionist, Parks's plays present us with an all-too-familiar world in which all human relations are monstrously transformed into abstractions and the money relation monstrously transformed into the only living reality, and ultimately into a divine entity. In investigating this theme, the plays also explore the involvement of money and economic thinking in ideas concerning representation, and specifically theatrical representation. Both plays wrestle with and ultimately try to transcend the logic of naturalism, a logic that represses money and one that would divide life into neat categories such as words and action, the mimetic and the real. Parks's own mélange of Brechtian and naturalistic theatrical practice attempts to arrive at a synthesis of these two lenses, one that would reject the logic of naturalism by acknowledging a dialectical relation between the symbolic and the real, that returns the body to language and language to the body, that writes "in the blood."

A close reading of *In the Blood* reveals first that the world it presents us with is one in which all relationships between characters are mediated by money, in a way that seems to make any kind of existentially authentic relationship between characters impossible. The character called Welfare explains to Hester that she "cares" about her "because it is my job to care. I am paid to stretch out these hands" (55). Reverend D, the preacher who fathered Hester's youngest child, runs a "salvation business" and explains at one point that most people think of God as "like the IRS. God garnishes yr wages if you dont pay up. God withholds" (73). The very antipathy felt by the general public toward Hester the supposed "welfare queen" is testament to the dominance of money in relations between people: in the last scene a chorus demands the sterilization of Hester based on economics: "NO SMART/ WOMAN GOT ALL THEM BASTARDS/ AND NOT A PENNY TO HER NAME/ SOMETHINGS GOTTA BE DONE/ CAUSE I'LL BE DAMNED IF SHE GONNA LIVE OFF ME" (109). Parks interrogates this idea of the "welfare queen" having children so she can receive money in the form of public assistance by having Hester refer to her children repeatedly as her "treasures" – indeed, this term, repeated three times, is Hester's first word in the play (12). The fact that Hester means something very different than the term's monetary interpretation only underscores the way financial value has supplanted all other forms of value for the play's other characters.

Another way of describing the role of money in the lives of the play's characters is to say that it has transformed from the ultimate *means* to the ultimate *end,* and in doing so has transformed all other contents of life into means to the end of making money. On the face of it this may seem a rather obvious point, but Parks powerfully brings us back to the truly monstrous nature of this situation through the character Amiga Gringa, Hester's "friend" and the only definitively white character in the play. Repeatedly, Amiga justifies her real and intended actions by appealing to the idea of the "open market." When, in scene five, Hester shows Amiga the sewing piece-work she has been offered by the character called Welfare, Amiga immediately suggests they steal the fabric and sell it "on the open market," as this will surely bring them more money than Hester could earn through sewing (67). In this same scene, Amiga reveals that she thinks she may be pregnant, and proposes to sell the baby. By the logic of the "free market" Amiga's intentions are perfectly reasonable, and she challenges the audience to consider this: "Grow it./ Birth it./ Sell it./ And why shouldn't I?" she asks rhetorically (71). According to Amiga, this arrangement makes particular sense because she is white: "Do you have any idea how much cash I'll get for the fruit of my white womb?" (71). The sickness of this economic perspective – but also the horrifyingly straightforward "logic" of it – are emphasized by Amiga's frank assessment of her situation: "Little Bastards in there living high on the hog, taking up space" (70). In a world where everyone is thought to be driven purely by economic interest, a fetus becomes a parasite living off the mother in much the same way that Hester becomes a parasite living off the public. Hester is accused of having children in order to make money, and Amiga's planned abortion makes economic sense, as would bringing the child to term and selling it. The point of each example is that human life, even from the perspective of a mother toward her child, is here no more than a means to the end of making money.

In The Blood thus sets up a kind of reproductive economy, one that demands that Hester be sterilized, as she is by the end of the play, presumably because the fruit of her *black* womb does not command the same price as would a white baby. Children are similarly seen as no more than a financial liability by the Reverend D, who tells us he gave Hester money for an abortion when he learned that she was pregnant with his child, and who explains to Hester in Scene Six that it would be financially ruinous for him to be seen with Hester since it would likely cause his financial "backers" to withhold the funds with which he hopes to build his church (75). The relation of money to reproduction is an ancient idea, one at the heart of what Aristotle characterized as money's monstrous quality. Aristotle's notion of money breeding money informs *In The Blood.* As Amiga's comments demonstrate, in this play, money reproduces itself *at the expense* of human reproduction: Amiga's baby is a parasite living off her limited financial resources – her "taking up space" comment essentially re-imagines the womb as real estate – only valuable if it can be *sold.* Similarly, Reverend D demonstrates the monstrous deformity of money's power – given his constant surveillance by his financial "backers" it makes greater economic sense for the Reverend to either eliminate his progeny (he says he has given Hester money to abort their child) or else distance himself from Hester and refuse to acknowledge the child.

Reverend D's vigilance concerning the maintenance of what Hester calls "his image" (99) underscores a more specific – and more insidious – effect of money in this play. Repeatedly, money is shown to demand a performance; it is consistently associated in the play with the construction and constant maintenance of a kind of mask, with characters' alienation from each other and, more disturbingly, from their own actions. Amiga Gringa explains in her "confession" that the sex show she had convinced Hester to take part in was financially "lucrative" because of Hester's ability to alienate herself from her own actions. "She liked the idea of sex," Amiga tells us, then adds, "at least she acted like it." She "had the moves down," which seems to describe a rote performance more than an authentic sexual encounter – a performance that was "very sensual, very provocative, very scientific, very lucrative" (72). These four consecutive adjectives trace a phenomenology of alienation, taking us from Hester's body, to a self-consciousness regarding the effect of the sex on an audience, to the "scientific" abstraction of her actions, and finally to money. Reverend D evinces a similar alienation from himself, and once again the root of that alienation is money: in the Reverend's case, his need to keep up a performance for financial backers who seem always to have him under their watchful gaze. As he explains to Hester, his patrons "want to make sure they havent been suckered, so they watch you real close, to make sure yr as good as they think you are. To make sure you wont screw up and shame them and waste their money" (75). Just as importantly, the good Reverend *is not* as good as they think he is – in the course of the play he masturbates in public, demands oral sex from Hester, and finally becomes physically abusive, calls Hester "Slut," and threatens to "crush [her] underfoot"(103). The Reverend is intensely conscious of a gap between appearance and reality, and it is money that makes this gap necessary.

Given the total replacement of all value by financial value in the world of Parks's play, and given money's evocation of a troubling gap between the symbolic and the real, it is natural that so many characters demonstrate a desperate need to close this gap, or sometimes to deny that this gap exists. The chorus of people whose shouts begin and end the play demonstrate just this denial. "BAD NEWS IN HER BLOOD," they shout at Hester, "PLAIN AS DAY" (7). Philip Kolin usefully points out that blood "symbolizes Hester's sexual sins and shame" and constitutes "her biological scarlet letter" (253). The chorus's accusation paradoxically both acknowledges and denies a gulf between the symbolic and the real: an essentialist claim is made about Hester's character – her fate is contained *in her blood* – but that writing (and it is called "news" after all) may be read clearly on the surface. Thus is Hester used to allay other characters' anxiety regarding what they sense is a discrepancy between the symbolic and the real.

An important way this anxiety concerning appearance and reality in a hypercommodified world is shown in the play is through problems of identity and identification. Reverend D, that walking symbol of this anxiety, begins his first soapbox sermon of the play with the words "You all know me. You know this face. You know these arms. This body of mine is known to you. To all of you. There isnt a person on the street tonight that hasnt passed me by at some point" (46). These statements are highly ironic given that the rest of the sermon concerns self-transformation, his own and that he promises to others who follow his advice. The Reverend even refers at one point to his "more recent reincarnation" (46). The latent content of the sermon then becomes the difficulty of *knowing* anyone. The very physical markers of identity cited by the Reverend – his face, his body – are highly unreliable symbols given his own admitted reincarnations and his need to maintain a false persona under the surveillance of his patrons.

In The Blood's other powerful symbol of the malleability of identity is Chilli, the father of Hester's oldest child who returns in scene seven with a changed name. When Hester reminds Chilli that she has protected him by not letting Welfare know he was back in town, since he has avoided paying Hester any child support, Chilli responds: "Theyll never find me. Theres no trace of the old me left anywhere" (87). Like Reverend D, Chilli has shed one self and adopted another, and as in the other man's case, Chilli's self-transformation is associated with money: "Ive seen the world Ive made some money Ive made a new name for myself," explains Chilli (89). These men whose money Hester so desperately needs (and is entitled to) have become money themselves, evincing just the break between seeming and being, face and material value money has come to symbolize.

Chilli's behavior allows Parks to further investigate money as a site of rupture between the symbolic and the real through the character's desperate need to place his own subjective/"interior" perception in accord with "objective" reality. In his desperate need for a correspondence between objective reality and his own subjective vision, Chilli resembles *The Scarlet Letter's* Chillingworth. When he is first introduced in the novel, he is described as "a man chiefly accustomed to look inward, and to whom external matters are of little value or import, unless they bear relation to something within his mind" (Hawthorne 44). In Parks's play, this need for clear correspondence between subjective perception and objective reality takes the form of what Chilli says his doctor labels a "tic" that is a "sure sign of some disorder" (87): he repeatedly and obsessively checks a gold pocket watch to try to verify his own subjective sense of what time it is. Chilli desperately needs to make the "real," objective world coincide with his subjective vision of it. He longs for what Goux suggests the American gold-money of the nineteenth century promised but could not possibly deliver: the erasure of difference between the real and the symbolic, a substance that *is* the value it *represents*. In fact the timepiece Chilli uses for this is a "big *gold* pocket watch" (67, emphasis added).

Chilli further attempts to make the real coincide with the symbolic when he dresses Hester in a wedding gown and declares, "This is real. The feelings I have for you, the feelings you are feeling for me, these are real" (92). He associates money with the denial of these feelings he wants certified as "real": he tells Hester "Ive been fighting my feelings for years. With every dollar I made" (92). As it turns out, the real is the very last thing Chilli is prepared to face. He tells Hester that he has "carried this picture of you. Sad and lonely with our child on yr hip. Struggling to make do. Struggling against all odds. And triumphant. Triumphant against everything. Like—hell, like Jesus and Mary" (96). Of course, when the actual Hester does not conform to his idealized vision, he rejects her with the explanation, "times change" – in fact another way of saying that *people* change. Chilli leaves, presumably to make more money and yet another "name" for himself.

The obsession over a perceived disjunction between symbols and the real demonstrated by the characters of *In The Blood* is transcended by only one character in the play, and that is – ironically – Hester's intellectually "slow" son Jabber. In the first scene following the opening chorus, we see two crucial and interrelated exchanges between Jabber and his illiterate mother. The first is a discussion of a word that someone has scrawled on Hester's "practice space," where she works at the alphabet Jabber tries to teach her. Hester's first words form the question as to whether it is "uh good word or a bad word" (9). The word, as the audience can see, is "SLUT," and Parks has Jabber respond with *no* words, but rather two "Spells," those wordless moments Parks has described as "heightened and elongated" pauses wherein characters "experience their pure true simple state" (ix). Hester pushes her eldest son to say the word so that the two of them can "figure out the meaning together" (9). Jabber resists because he knows what the word means, or at least he knows that it is a "bad word." Crucially, Jabber understands the word as an *action,* one meant to have a very real effect on his mother: "They wrote it in yr practice place," he observes, "so you didn't practice today" (10).

Unlike other characters in this play, Jabber clearly understands the slipperiness of the talk/ action distinction, understands, that is, that talk *is* action, that symbols are involved in the creation of the real and vice versa. A moment later when Hester tries to make an A in the dirt, Jabber makes a correction by using the body: "Legs apart hands crost the chest like I showd you" (11). Then Hester pushes Jabber again to "Read that word out to me," and Jabber lies, saying he "Cant" (11). These two exchanges – regarding the "bad" word Jabber refuses to say aloud and the method Jabber uses to teach Hester the alphabet – are vitally related in that both refuse to recognize a hard distinction between talk and action, symbolic and real. The first registers the real effects of a symbol, and the second searches for a kind of embodied – we might even say performed – language.[19]

A bit later in the same scene Hester does sense that the word is a "mean ugly" one "meant to hurt our feelings" (12). In response to this, Jabber seems to deny the knowledge he has already demonstrated regarding the slipperiness of the real/symbolic distinction: referencing the old "Sticks and stones" saw, Jabber insists, "Words don't hurt my feelings" (12). Then immediately the word/action distinction is revisited when Hester's daughter Bully enters telling her mother that her brother Trouble "said a bad word" that she will not repeat, then notes "What he said was bad but what he did, what he did was worse" (we soon learn that Trouble has stolen a policeman's club) (13).

An interrogation of the talk/action distinction haunts other plays by Parks, most notably *Topdog/Underdog.* This theme is revisited at the very climax of *In the Blood,* again in a scene focusing on Hester and Jabber. Crucially, this scene occurs just after the Reverend D viciously calls Hester "Slut," verbalizing the written word we see near the beginning of the play. In scene 8, having heard the Reverend D's verbal abuse of Hester, Jabber admits that he could have read the word aloud to her but "didn't wanna" (103). In a nice reversal, Hester now tells Jabber not to speak, but the two have an extraordinary exchange in which Jabber reveals the depth of his understanding about the relation of the symbolic to the real. "I was reading" the word, explains Jabber, "but I was only reading it in my head I wasn't reading it with my mouth I was reading it with my mouth but not with my tongue I was reading it only with my lips and I could hear the word outloud but only outloud in my head" (103). Jabber explains to Hester that he "didnt wanna say the word outloud in your head" (104). It is remarkable how the "bad" word moves, in Jabber's speech, from his own subjectivity, through his body (his mouth, his tongue), out into the air and then into his mother's subjectivity: Jabber saying the word "outloud in [Hester's] head." Jabber has a sophisticated understanding of the fluid relation between "inside" and "outside," between subjectivity and objectivity. Through the character of Jabber, Parks replaces a hard distinction between talk and action, the symbolic and the real, with a more sophisticated understanding of the two as dialectically interrelated.

The ultimate demonstration of the involvement of the symbolic in the real is the tragic, bloody murder of Jabber by his own mother. Hester brutally slays her son to stop him saying the hurtful word. What's more, the weapon Hester uses is the policeman's club that Trouble stole at the beginning of the play (the deed his sister Bully uses to distinguish between words – the "bad" word Trouble said – and actions). That club becomes the means by which Hester would control the real by limiting the "talk" of other characters. Interestingly, by the time of the killing of Jabber, the stolen policeman's club has already been involved in the play's meditations on the question of free will. In Scene Four, for instance, Hester twice warns Welfare, "Dont make me hurt you," the second time raising the club to hit her (57, 58). The phrase speaks to Hester's own feeling of powerlessness by denying her agency even in this imagined striking out against her oppressors. In fact repeatedly in the play Hester's language reveals her own perceived lack of agency. "We ain't lucky," Hester declares early in the play, and she repeatedly mentions an always-elusive "leg up" that will help her children and herself, maybe even "make us rich, " though she acknowledges that there is "no easy money nowheres" (12, 58, 64). "I coulda been the Queen of Sheba," Hester tells the Doctor in scene two, only "it just werent in the cards" (41). Parks is not blaming Hester for the character's own perceived lack of agency. To read the play in this way is to ignore both the notably rigid hierarchy that encompasses all of the characters as well as the play's consistent undermining of Reverend D's manipulative, dishonest "self-help" philosophy. The Doctor who eventually sterilizes Hester does so, he says, at the behest of "The Higher Ups" (41). In fact, in the monologues called "Confessions" that punctuate the play, various characters – the Doctor, the Reverend, Amiga, Welfare – confess to their own lack of agency. "Times are tough," says the Doctor in a typical passage, "What can we do?" (44). Amiga Gringa justifies Hester's exploitation this way: "Ah, what do you expect in a society based on Capitalizm?" (72). And the Reverend D lives under the constant surveillance of his "backers." All of these characters consistently blame Hester for her own situation while all deny any agency on their own part.

This sense of inevitability finds its ultimate symbol in *In the Blood* in the form of cosmic signs Hester repeatedly reports observing. In Scenes Five and Six, Hester claims to have seen an eclipse, though other characters claim not to have seen it (66, 76). By Scene Seven the eclipse has become a "Big dark thing. Gods hand. Coming down on me. Blocking the light out" and even the "5-fingered hand of fate" (84). Scene Eight, in which Hester kills Jabber, is entitled "The Hand of Fate" (99), and Hester's last words – also the last words of the play – are "Big hand coming down on me" repeated three times (110). None of the other characters see the hand but, as we've argued, they all seem to live with the sense of helplessness and lack of agency the hand of fate symbolizes. This is a lack of agency rooted in economic thinking. In the world of the play, what Aristotle called the unnatural "breeding of money" has been made natural, and the "breeding" of humans been made unnatural: a baby is either a way to make money (as Amiga sees it) or a financial burden on society (as Hester is seen). Hester's "spaying" *for economic reasons* is the ultimate, monstrous end of this process of reification. The "hand of fate" that no one but Hester sees is Smith's "Invisible Hand," that force born of self-interest, competition, and supply and demand.

As in *In The Blood,* in *Fucking A* we are presented with a world in which characters seem forced to profit off each other's misfortunes. Unsurprisingly in this bloody revenge tragedy that Parks coyly refers to as an "otherworldly tale," the situation is even more vicious, the characters' sense of helplessness even more pronounced (113). In the first scene of the play, Hester Smith describes the situation this way, in reference to her abortion business: "Their troubles yr livelihood, [. . .] There aint no winning" (117). Similarly, the character called Freedom Fund decries the loose sexual morals of the women of the town but then throws her hands up and asks "what can you do?" since "them cleaning up their act would put you out of yr cleaning business" (132). And Hester's best friend, Canary, who would have the Mayor as her husband and financial benefactor at any cost, celebrates his troubled marriage: "Things are getting worse between the Mayor and his wife. Lets celebrate" (119). Later in the play Canary tells Hester she has a story to tell that will "make you smile" since "Its at her expense" (123). With one notable exception, which I shall discuss, the characters of *Fucking A* always and everywhere profit at each others' expense while remaining convinced of their own lack of agency.

While *In The Blood* implicates the money relation in characters' widespread lack of agency, *Fucking A* gives us what at least appears to be a more stable system of money: money is tied to gold, and there only seem to be two denominations of currency, gold pieces (presumably gold coins) and what are just called "coins," with one of the former equaling 500 of the latter. In this way the money economy of *Fucking A* resembles the gold-money economy of nineteenth-century America. Helpfully, Jean-Joseph Goux traces a vital homology between what Marx calls the three historical stages of money –measure of labor, medium of exchange, and finally means of wealth – and the psychoanalytic categories of the real, the symbolic, and the imaginary. Like Marc Shell, Goux cites the gold-money of the nineteenth century as an instance of the fantasy of bringing these three functions together in one object: "At once the *ideal* measure of value, the *symbolic* instrument of exchange, and the *real* means of reserve, gold-money brought together the functions of *archetype,* of *token,* and of *treasure* into a single object." Yet with the advent of representative money (paper, then credit cards, then electronic money), the "three functions have come asunder":

> The inconvertible signifier that circulates today, that floats, that always postpones its 'realization,' guarantees the monetary function in the realm of pure symbolicity, but only by mourning the loss of the unlocatable (or floating) standard and the uncertain reserve value, secured by nothing. (114)

The money system of *Fucking A* seemingly represents just the fantasy of a value that *is* what it *represents* that gold (and silver) money represented to the "hard" money advocates of the American nineteenth century. A closer look at the play, however, reveals that in the play as in life, the real value of money is just as relative despite its being tied to gold. We see this most clearly through Hester's attempts to buy visitation rights to her imprisoned son Boy. Each time Hester saves up enough money to purchase a picnic with Boy, the price of that picnic changes due to further crimes Boy has supposedly committed while in prison, and Hester falls short. When she shows up with a gold coin to purchase visitation rights, she is told that due to further crimes committed by Boy, his "picnic price has doubled" (134). Though Hester's son, as we learn, likely has been involved in further crimes, the rather arbitrary and extreme changes in the cost of his visitation rights undermine any supposedly stabilizing character of the gold-money.

The play goes further to implicate money in the relativizing of all other value and meaning in the world of the characters. When, in scene six, Canary is crushed to learn that even if the Mayor has his wife murdered, he will not marry Canary, the Mayor assuages her disappointment by giving her gold (153). Then after each character has a "Spell," the Mayor says "'Wife,' 'Mistress,' what does it matter? Take the gold. Buy something nice" (153). Money erases the difference between wife and mistress. As soon as Canary has the money, she does an immediate emotional about-face, calling the Mayor "Sweetheart" and then breaking into the song "Gilded Cage" (153). Likewise, the First Lady, desperate to get pregnant for what basically amount to economic reasons, erases the difference between two ostensibly very different people – her husband the Mayor and the escaped convict Monster (who in reality is Hester's son Boy). Happy to discover that she is pregnant with Monster's baby, and deciding to let the Mayor think it is his, she reasons: "One seed is as good as another. And when the husband resembles the lover, he wont be none the wiser" (191). The economic ends, here, constitute what is important, and they make human beings interchangeable.

As the world of *Fucking A* seems at first to have a less monstrous money form, so does that world seem to regulate semiotic exchanges through a kind of hierarchical system. To begin with, there are two different kinds of spoken English in the play: "ordinary" speech and TALK, a special language that for the most part only the women use when speaking to each other. Although Talk is a strange sort of English-German-novel language, one thing that is clear is that it is much more concrete and metaphorical than the standard English used by most of the characters most of the time. Parks provides a TALK-English translation at the back of the printed play. Menstruation is expressed in TALK as "falltimeh ma OVO" (124); and the First Lady compliments the state of her own vagina in similarly concrete, imagistic language: "Meh Kazo-say greengrass ee-sunny skies" (128). After TALK, there is the comparatively less metaphor-rich, less concretely expressive standard English most of the characters use. Finally there is writing, most of which is done by a character called Scribe, who in one instance in the play takes down Hester's words in a letter to her imprisoned son. Hester freely admits that this letter contains lies (148), leaving us to wonder if, in the world of the play, lying becomes easier the further speech moves from the body.

Given this question concerning the relation of truth to the present, speaking body, two further semiotic levels must be considered. The first involves identifying marks on the physical body: the marks Hester created to ensure that she would always recognize her son (two identical scars she created with her teeth, on her son's arm and on her own, "in the same place"), as well as the letter "A" that has been branded into Hester's chest (166). The next semiotic level involves the embodied/performed, non-verbal communication that Parks refers to as "Spells." If *In The Blood* began with its protagonist embodying the letter A and ended with her writing in blood, thus evincing a concern with bridging the gap between the immediate presence of the body and the absence of writing, the later play further investigates this idea through these different semiotic levels that exist in different proximities to the physical body. Given that Parks describes a Spell as a non-verbal means of communicating a character's "pure true simple state" (ix), it is not unreasonable to assume that a continuum exists in this play wherein the truth becomes more obscured as we move from the performing body, to writing on the body, to private language (TALK), to public discourse, and finally to writing, or words separated from a speaker.

While on one level it seems that Parks is setting up this hierarchy of semiotic economies, with symbols becoming less reliable the further removed they are from the body, in fact the play deeply complicates this hierarchy. One way this is done is through Hester's repeated failure to recognize her own son. When, in scene nine, Butcher suggests that Hester likely won't be able to recognize her son, not having seen him since he was a small child, Hester reveals that she has already anticipated this problem. "[J]ust before they took him," she explains, "I bit him. Hard. Right on the arm just there. I bit hard. Deep into his skin. His blood in my mouth" (166). Hester then bit an "identical" mark into her own arm. In this way Hester resists the tendency of the commodification of life to reduce all to least common denominator, to make all interchangeable – to erase the difference between "wife" and "mistress," for example – by giving her son a distinctive mark. At the same time, however, the identical marks Hester places on her son's and her own body symbolize Hester's refusal to see her son as a separate, distinct, existentially independent being. She would have him always be the "angel" she once convinced herself he was, and no amount of evidence of his violent acts will change this view of him. The mark by which Hester tries to make her son always recognizable to her is also the mark by which she tries to fix his identity to match her own ideal vision of it. The two scars are, in an interesting way, very like the scarlet A in Hawthorne's tale, in that all three symbols try to make a supposed "internal"/spiritual/ideal state externally visible, or they all three try to place the real and the symbolic in sync. Hester Smith even says of her own scar that it "[k]ind of looks like a heart. Like Im wearing my heart on my sleeve or something" (179). The very scar, then, that would fix Boy's identity in fact marks the dissolution of that identity in the face of Hester's idealized image of her son.

In her need for a simple and reliable correspondence between "inside" and "outside," the real and the symbolic, the Hester of *Fucking A* actually resembles Chili from *In the Blood.* Chili obsessed over his need to make the external world coincide with his own idealized vision of it – we saw this through his compulsive game with his pocket watch and his rejection of Hester La Negrita when she refused to conform to his idealized vision of her. Similarly, Hester Smith would erase the difference between the symbolic and the real, and refuses to recognize physical reality when it does not coincide with her own idealized vision. When Freedom Fund tells Hester her son has committed more crimes in prison, Hester responds "Must be a mistake. Hes a very good boy" (133). Freedom Fund's response would subtly move identity from essence to existence: "Well, yr good boys been doing some very bad things lately" (133). Yet Hester insists, "My sons an angel" (134). The character called Butcher possesses the same essentialist view of his own daughter, except that instead of seeing her as an "angel" he calls her "[r]otten to the core" (160).

A powerful irony of the play is that it is just this refusal on Hester's part to let go of an essentialist view of identity that keeps her from recognizing her own son. When Canary points out that Monster, the recently escaped convict, has a scar very like Hester's, Hester refuses to believe this could be her son, saying "Hes an evil person" (196). When Canary reminds her again about the identical scars, Hester makes the following leap: "Which goes to show that mothers all over the world bite their sons" (196). Hester's inability to let go of her own idealized image of her son makes the recognition she sought to enable with the scar impossible. Monster's scar, insists Hester, "looks horrid. Like a gash," while hers "looks like a heart" (209). It is easier for Hester to believe that her son is dead than it is for her to accept that he is not the "angel" she repeatedly swears he is. When Monster shows her his mark, Hester responds, "I marked my *son.* He was good and then he died" (208). This narrative Hester constructs and clings to about her son denies that son as a living, acting being. He *was good* – a description of an essential state, not an action – and then he died.

Tragically, Hester's inability to see people as complex beings that change over time is at the very root of the revenge fantasy that drives the plot of *Fucking A.* After all, Hester holds the First Lady responsible for "snitching" on Boy *when she was a little girl.* Unwilling or unable to blame the legal system for turning her Boy into a "Monster," for essentially holding him for ransom through its "Freedom Fund," Hester simply persists in blaming the person whose initial act sent Boy to prison in the first place. Crucially, money is deeply involved in Hester's obsession with the First Lady. In the first scene of the play, Hester explains that "When she was a little Rich Girl she thought she owned the world. And anything she wanted she could buy. Sent my son away to prison with a flick of her little Rich Girl finger" (124). Now, however, the First Lady is thought (incorrectly) to be infertile, and Hester takes pleasure in this fact: "She cant buy a son or a daughter now but I can buy mine. Im buying mine back" (124). Two things are significant here. The first is that, as in *In The Blood,* the money economy here seems to flourish at the expense of the human reproductive economy. The "Rich Girl" has no offspring, while the financially strapped Hester does. The second interesting thing is that Hester would take comfort in the very quality that makes human life convertible into money. The same money economy that grants the Mayor the "exclusive rights" of another human being (his mistress, Canary), that makes the difference between wife and mistress meaningless, that puts a price on Hester's son's freedom, also allows Hester the only hope she has of ever reuniting with that son. This *all-encompassing* quality of the money economy is the real tragedy of *Fucking A.* Hester is of course deluded in thinking she could use that money economy to get her son back, as the price of even a visit escalates astronomically and continually. The point is that she is allowed no other option: that money is seen as the only available and always insufficient means of overcoming the very alienation that it has created.

The comfort Hester derives from the First Lady's supposed sterility dissipates when it is discovered that the First lady is in fact pregnant. When Hester has her nemesis drugged and brought to her home and then performs an abortion on the woman, she unwittingly destroys her own grandchild. If Hester had not chased her son off immediately before the First Lady's arrival, having refused to recognize him even after he showed her his "mark," this final, tragic mistake would have been avoided. In an important sense, however, Hester's insistence on revenge is a powerful rejection of the money economy and all it represents in the play. Earlier, when it is believed that Hester's son is dead, Canary advises Hester to just accept an offered "full refund" of all the money she has contributed over the years toward buying a visit with her son, get over her hatred of the First Lady, and retire. Canary suggests they should both "take [their] bad luck on the chin" and move on, but Hester insists on having her revenge, despite Canary's sense of powerlessness ("Anyway, what can we do?" asks Canary rhetorically) (194). Here Hester refuses to be paid off in cash and rejects the lack of agency the money economy encourages throughout the play. The life of her son, insists Hester, can never be valued in money: "A full refund aint enough" (195).

At the same time as she refuses to put a price on her son's life, the very logic of Hester's revenge demonstrates her conditioning by the money economy, with its demand that all be reduced to a least common denominator. Hester first plans to kill the First Lady, an action she says would make them "equal" (193). Obviously this would not, in any meaningful sense, make them equal, since Hester is still alive. When Hester learns of the First Lady's pregnancy, she hits on the idea of getting her due by aborting the fetus: "Rip her child from her like she ripped mine from me" (205). Of course, the real situation is more complicated than this, and the First Lady, whatever her faults, did not "rip" Hester's child from her. This careless thinking equates two very disparate things as monstrously as money does, and the results are tragic for Hester: she unwittingly aborts her own grandson and also loses precious time during which she might have saved her son from a group of vicious bounty hunters. Hester declares that she is "not a mother" if she foregoes vengeance on the First Lady (194). The end result is that she is no longer a mother *as a result of* her insistence on settling the score, on *paying back* the First Lady in kind.

Hester's last act is to slit the throat of her son using a method Butcher taught her, one he uses to kill the animals which exist for him only as commodities. The most remarkable thing about Hester's mercy killing of her own son is the utter meaningless of it. One is tempted to read this act as at least marking Hester's agency, but that begs the question, of what use is agency such as this? Her Boy is denied dignity even in death, as the Hunters declare there is "[p]lenty of fun still to be had" with his body (220). The extent of the Hunters's own inability to think "outside" the money economy is shown in the First Hunter's comment, to a woman who has just killed her own son: "If you think yll get any of the reward money, you got another thing coming" (220). Hester tries to sing another verse of her "Working Woman's Song," that paean to her lack of agency in the capitalist world of the play: "I dig my ditch with no complaining," the song begins (221). Hester does trail off, seemingly unable to finish the song, but in the end she "*gets up, picks up her tools and goes back to work,*" Parks's stage directions tell us. No significant change, either for Hester or for any of the other surviving characters, seems to have occurred as a result of the actions of the play.

In both *In The Blood* and *Fucking A,* Hester's murder of her own son is deeply involved with her desperate attempt to escape being objectively determined by her respective society, and in each play it is the money relation that is implicated in the protagonist's sense of being objectively determined. And in both plays, the protagonist remains just as trapped and powerless as she was in the beginning. Elam is correct in seeing Hester La Negrita's murder of Jabber as a striking out against a social order that "not only restricts the roles of women and people of color, but also preordains how one's offspring will function within this system," (203). Nevertheless, as Verna Foster usefully points out, that the two Hesters ultimately harm those they love and themselves "without effecting any change in the social conditions that produced their rages" (75). Despite her son Jabber's lessons on the mutually generative relationship between human subjectivity and what we perceive as the objective world, Hester La Negrita ends the play succumbing to what she perceives as the "Hand of Fate." Despite her own struggle to escape the money relation and its tendency to make all interchangeable, Hester Smith is still resigned to a fate that is beyond her control. In this way the Red Letter plays seem to suggest an extremely pessimistic view of humans' ability to wrest control of their own lives from the very market mechanisms they have created.

Yet this view of the plays as confirming their protagonists' view of their own helplessness is only possible if we ignore Parks's masterful employment of Brechtian stagecraft.[20] Both plays make use of Brechtian devices such as episodic plotting, single actors playing multiple roles, songs, figurative names (Trouble, Jabber, Monster, Welfare), onstage text (the doctor's mortarboard in *In The Blood;* the "nonaudible simultaneous English translation" of the TALK passages that Parks's stage directions call for in *Fucking A)* (115). In addition, Parks's novel use of the chorus in *In The Blood* similarly creates a very Brechtian combination of distance and identification for the audience. Harvey Young notes that through her "embrace and (post)modernization of the Greek chorus," Parks uses that chorus as a "veiled critique of present-day, societal complicity in the objectification of others" (30). The audience recognizes itself in the chorus but does not like what it sees. Through all these Brechtian devices, Parks discourages our over-identification with the heroines of the two plays, rejects the classical idea of the characters' *hamartia* as responsible for their fate, and works against realism's tendency to encourage a view of the world as always already pre-constructed. The "fate" of Parks's two Hesters demonstrates the folly of looking for a solution on the level of the individual. The Brechtian stagecraft works in conjunction with the plays' content to encourage us to work toward a structural solution to the problem the play foregrounds. And there are hints within the plays of the more humans social arrangements we might choose to construct, none more powerful than the one non-economic relationship in *In The Blood.* Hester and Canary may joke about the economics of their relationship – long ago Hester gave Canary an abortion on credit – but the truth about their relationship is very different. Hester says. Hester calls herself "a good business woman" for placing Canary in her debt. Canary, however, upon paying Hester her "debt and then some," tells the truth: "Yr a good friend" (126,125).

CHAPTER SEVEN

PROSPECTS: STAGING MONEY, AND A NOTE ON AUTHENTICITY

It is useful to take stock of what emerge as structural similarities in modern American dramatic treatments of economic life. In most of the plays in this study there is an agon between at least one character consumed with a desire to "escape" the money economy and at least one other character who uncannily embodies the very qualities of money that so disturb the former character. This is manifest most clearly in *American Buffalo,* where Don's anxieties concerning the lack of a "hard" distinction between talk and action, his inability to either engage in or speak of financial transactions, and his planned theft of the buffalo nickel legitimately purchased all speak to his inability to think outside a naturalist logic embodied by Teach, a character who both terrifies and tantalizes Don with the message that while Don can deal only in the soft currency of representations that have no relation to the gold standard of the real, he (Teach) somehow has transcendental access to that real: "Things are what they are," says Teach, who has come to face "facts" (8, 64).

In *Dead End* the need to both escape and embrace what money represents is similarly divided amongst contending male characters, but here the dual plotlines give us something slightly more complicated. Among the child characters, Tommy's deep anxiety concerning the tendency of appearances to deceive (an anxiety repeatedly associated, as we've seen, with money) finds its perfect manifestation in Spit, the Judas who "sells Tommy out" to the police. Spit represents an idea of "outward" appearances as totally divorced from "inner" or "essential" reality (a rejection of the innocent Dippy's notion that "[c]heatin' shows" [88]). Tommy's desperate desire is to "mark" Spit, making his *appearance* match his "essential" reality, ensuring that Spit, like the fantasy of gold money, *is* the value he *represents* (153). Among the adult characters, Pete Gimpty (like the young Tommy) is troubled by the difference between what's "inside" a person and what's "outside." As a walking representation of the unreliable and arbitrary relation of appearance to reality, the fully commodified, surgically altered gangster Baby-Face Martin (in this sense an adult version of Spit) embodies Gimpty's deepest anxieties. Just as Tommy would "mark" Spit, Gimpty must similarly limit the free-play of Martin-as-signifier (and as money). Gimpty achieves this by supplying the police with information that leads to their eventually killing Baby Face. This killing transforms Baby-Face into the only two realities allowed by the logic of naturalism: a physical, corporeal reality that refuses signification (Baby-Face's body as "chopped meat") and a "soft" currency not backed by a "hard" value: the dead Baby-Face's wad of bills (145). The two plots of *Dead End* finally come together through a third clash between one who would escape and one who would embody money. Still desperately resisting the arbitrary relation of appearance to the real that the play associates with money, the child-hero Tommy faces the adult-hero Gimpty, the latter now transformed (through the appropriation of Baby-Face's values and Baby-Face's money) into yet another avatar of the former's anxieties concerning money.

The male characters of *Death of a Salesman* are compelled by this same conflict between fleeing money and embodying it, though the consistent association of each position with an individual character is more complex. Willy's deep anxieties regarding money and the commodification of his own identity find their perfectly uncanny embodiment in his brother Ben. An immaterial ghost (and/or a hallucination) that nevertheless repeatedly invokes the notion of a "hard" value you can "lay your hands on," Ben, like Teach in *American Buffalo* and Baby-Face in *Dead End,* simultaneously evokes the two possibilities allowed by the logic of naturalism: an immanent, essential and unrepresentable value and an empty signifier (360). In the conflict between Willy and Biff, conversely, it is usually Willy who plays the role of uncanny embodiment of money. Through his compulsion to steal and his repeated attempts to enact a rural, western idyll, Biff desperately hopes to escape the world of money he associates with both his father and the city. Of course Biff and Willy also at times trade roles in relation to money, with Biff arguing that he and Willy are both "a dime a dozen" and Willy responding "I am not a dime a dozen! I am Willy Loman and you are Biff Loman!" (132). Finally both Biff and Willy at various moments in the play embody *both* a desire to escape and a desire to embrace money and what it represents in the play. This situation is seen in Biff's description of his repeated escape from and return to the city and the world of business, as well as in Willy's confrontation with his boss

Howard Wagner and his (Willy's) decision ultimately to kill himself; both these situations involve Willy's simultaneously arguing for a value as a commodity and a value as a "man."

In Wilson's *Joe Turner's Come and Gone,* Henry Loomis would escape a logic that "marks" him racially and economically. The businessman Seth here appears as the representative of this logic, with his insistence on the infallibility of his all-pervasive gaze, his belief in his own ability to "size up" people and situations, and his ignorance regarding the extent to which his own perception is mediated by his role as businessman and entrepreneur. As in *Death of a Salesman,* Wilson's play ends by acknowledging both a need to escape this economic thinking and a seeming impossibility to do so: Henry Loomis has attained a new sort of agency, but it is a dubious one considering he play's treatment of economic life: he is "shining like new money."

In *Topdog/Underdog* the younger brother Booth represents the attempt to escape the money economy, while the older brother Lincoln – that "Dead President" – embodies money. Booth's desperate insistence on a hard distinction between talk and action (or the mimetic and the authentic), his refusal to count or even verify the existence of his "inheritance," his constant stealing, and his inability to spend money all attest to the character's repression of money. Lincoln's obvious enjoyment in spending money; his tendency to problematize the distinction between talk and action, performativity and authenticity; and his association with Abe Lincoln and the bill that bears his name all associate that character with money and its dislocating effects. Booth views Lincoln-as-con-artist as the "authentic" Lincoln, and repeatedly urges his brother to be once again *who he really is.* At the same time, Booth believes he can change his own "essential" nature by simply changing his name. Unable or unwilling to learn his brother's lessons on the complex relation of signs to the real, soft money to hard specie, Booth *eliminates* this complexity by killing Lincoln, just as he threatens to kill anyone who will not call him by his new name – as in the other plays in this study, Booth's desperate need to control signs knows no bounds and ultimately ends in violence. As in *Dead End* and *Death of a Salesman, Topdog/Underdog* ends with the character associated with money transforming, through his death, into the two "sides of the coin" allowed by the logic of naturalism: a "hard" physical substance that does not signify, and those "soft" greenbacks.

The situation is somewhat more complicated in Parks's "Red Letter" Plays. In these works, most of the characters represent both the desperate desire to escape economies of money and of signs generally even as their alienated, shape-shifting, amoral ways represent just those economies.

The obsession with authenticity at the heart of the logic of naturalism seems by the early twentieth century to have reached some sort of critical mass. Nowhere, perhaps, is this more powerfully demonstrated than on the ubiquitous dramatic and commercial medium that is contemporary American television, where there has been an explosion in the last two decades of so-called "Reality" programming. Much of this programming, in fact, is highly naturalistic in its social-Darwinian emphasis on "weeding out" the "weak" members among a group, especially on shows like the hugely popular *Survivor*, which purports to return its competitors to a state of nature where they can test themselves to see "what they're made of." If these shows strive to recreate the same Crusoe-like, extremely self-interested survivalism of *homo economicus,* the model of human behavior underlying classical economics, other Reality shows feature men and women competing in a more explicitly economic realm, specifically in the world of business; shows like *The Apprentice* pit "normal" people against each other in cutthroat corporate settings. Other, less ostensibly competitive Reality shows like MTV's *The Real World* and BRAVO's *The Real Housewives of Orange County* purport to show "ordinary" people living ordinary lives. The "Real" worlds of these shows, of course, are always highly theatrical spaces: the "pimped-out" urban apartments and oversized imitation colonial McMansions that serve as the "real" settings of these programs are carnivalesque spaces that problematize the very idea of authenticity. As with the settings of these shows, so with their stars: they are for the most part anything but "normal" or "real," but seem instead chosen for their extremely melodramatic, self-consciously performative natures. In fact, several of the most recent incarnations of Reality TV place special emphasis on the carnivalesque and the monstrous: shows like *The Osbournes, Gene Simmons Family Jewels,* and *Hogan Knows Best* all have at their center a performer known for his circus-like performances – two from the world of "Heavy Metal" music, one from the even more carnivalesque world of professional wrestling – engaged in their own, updated versions of the "normal" family dramas that formed the conflicts of classic American family comedies like *Leave It To Beaver.* Now, however, it's all "real"; except that obviously, it isn't. Through highly manipulative editing, through the use of music and visual effects, and through the very choice of the people featured in the shows, a highly *unreal* "real" experience is guaranteed. The title of one of the newest of these programs gets it closest to correct: *The Surreal Life.* Surrealism itself functions to problematize the very distinction between the real and the mimetic, the authentic and the performative, uncannily foregrounding the ways we construct "reality" by giving a plasticity to psychological states and de-essentializing "hard" reality. Accordingly, *The Surreal Life* features a cast of "real" characters including, in addition to once-popular actors past their prime, a former porn star (Ron Jeremy), a former female wrestler (Chyna Doll), a washed-up white rapper (Vanilla Ice), and a washed-up black rapper (Flavor Flav). Each of these characters made a career out of essentially performing authenticity and authenticating performance, blurring the line between what's "real" and what's "fake." By now treating them as "real" people living together, having the same petty domestic squabbles everyone else has, the shows both encourage a critical eye toward the fetishization of celebrity, *and* foreground the performativity of "real" domestic life. Like the plays discussed in this study, Reality TV essentially presents us with monstrous versions of the American nuclear family, and in doing so just may encourage – despite itself – a more sophisticated conception of the relation between the authentic and the mimetic than it has so far been given credit for.

Recently, a growing number of cultural commentators are calling for just such a sophistication concerning the notion of the authentic and performance, decrying what Orlando Patterson recently called a "cult of authenticity."[21] The American obsession with who or what someone is "on the inside" or "in their heart," writes Patterson, now "dominates our way of viewing ourselves and our relationships, with baleful consequences. Within sensitive individuals it breeds doubt; between people it promotes distrust; within groups it enhances group-think in the endless quest to be one with the group's true soul; and between groups it is the inner source of identity politics." The search for the authentic also has serious political consequences. In America today, writes Patterson, it has lead to our preference for "leaders who feel our pain, or born-again frat boys who claim that they can stare into the empty eyes of an ex-K.G.B. agent and see inside his soul" (A35). One cannot help but be reminded of Ronald Reagan's famous line, regarding his involvement in the Iran-Contra affair, that while his "heart" told him he was innocent, "the facts" told another story. Reagan (or his speechwriters) knew his audience, and it was always clear to the true believers which they should trust: slippery "facts" or the authentic, never-changing "heart."

The antidote to all this, according to Patterson, is first distinguishing between "sincerity" and authenticity, and then settling for the former in "non-intimate and secular relations." Patterson's view of sincere – as opposed to authentic – social relations is essentially performative: "Its iconic expression is the celebrated passage from Shakespeare: 'All the world's a stage,/ And all the men and women merely players./ They have their exits and their entrances,/ And one man in his time plays many parts'" (qtd. In Patterson A35). Yet Patterson elides obvious difficulties here when he enjoins us to "act and really be the way that we present ourselves to others" (A35). The question this begs is the very question that Kingsley, Miller, Mamet, Wilson, and Parks are trying to work out: how does one *act* and also *really be?* The answer, if there is one, lies somewhere beyond the logic of gold money, real TV, and realistic drama, though they all begin to point a way. It would be an answer that makes a line from the "Best Customer" of Parks's *Topdog/Underdog* more than a comment on our culture of narcissism, but an ontological musing on the complex interrelation of performance and the real, the mimetic and the authentic: "Does thuh show stop when no ones watching or does thuh show go on" (39)?

NOTES

[1] In 1932 alone, 273,000 Americans lost their homes (Siracusa and Coleman 13).

[2] The "welfare statists," writes Greenspan, "have created paper reserves in the form of government bonds which – through a complex series of steps – the banks accept in place of tangible assets and treat as if they were an actual deposit of gold" (94).

[3] For a survey of economists' statements on the 1930s gold-standard debate, see Hoeller.

[4] Despite its success, *Dead End* is best remembered today – when it is remembered at all – as the basis for the film of the same title directed by William Wyler from a screenplay by Lillian Hellman. And that film's reputation has survived largely due to its launching the careers of the group of child actors known first as the "Dead End Kids" (in films such as the 1938 James Cagney classic "Angels with Dirty Faces") and later as the "East Side Kids," the "Little Tough Guys" and finally the "Bowery Boys" (in a string of film comedies).

[5] Kay's pragmatic rejection of Gimpty is illustrated more powerfully in the film version of *Dead End.* We see Kay attempt to ascend a squalid staircase to reach Gimpty's tenement flat, then flee in disgust before she can bring herself to enter Gimpty's apartment.

[6] After tripping and nearly jabbing a prostrate Biff in the eye with the point of his umbrella, Ben admonishes Willy's son: "Never fight fair with a stranger, boy. You'll never get out of the jungle that way" (Miller 49).

[7] Ben's first response to Willy's question is both less forthcoming and more indicative of Ben's use for "talk": "Oh, there's a story in that" (Miller 47).

[8] The metaphor of business as war is still very much with us, as war "manuals" such as Sun Tzu's *The Art of War* are routinely adapted for use by business professionals.

[9] As Simmel points out, an all-encompassing desire for the object could lead to theft, which is effectively the end of the economic system and thus of all economic value.

[10] Eisinger (mistakenly, in my view) sees *Salesman* as romanticizing the American agrarian myth.

[11] For criticism focusing on the talk/action distinction in Mamet's work, see especially King, Worster, and Dean. Piette makes the point that "most of these critics argued that the three characters in the play engage in sterile logorrhea instead of proceeding with the planned robbery precisely because, for them, talk is action" (92).

[12] Freud describes a game he witnessed his grandson play (12–17). The boy would cast a wooden toy away from him, then pull it back by a string that was attached. Freud interpreted the sounds the boy made as fort (gone) and da (here) and hypothesized that he was dealing with his inability to control the presence or absence of his mother by controlling the presence or absence of the toy.
[13] For a more thorough exploration of the subject of *laissez-faire* capitalism in *American Buffalo,* see Callens.
[14] Mary L. Bogumil has commented on the strangeness of Wilson's introduction, but only to mention that the author "personifies many elements of the setting" in order to emphasize the sense of displacement the black characters feel in the North. My own interpretation acknowledges this as well, but goes a bit further to see the description as partaking of the economic reification of the naturalist mode.
[15] For what it's worth, there is also a five-year difference in the ages of the brothers.
[16] The roles of Lincoln and Booth, in this regard, are very similar to the roles of Teach and Don in Mamet's *American Buffalo*; in each pair, the former emerges as the perfectly uncanny manifestation of the latter's deepest anxieties regarding economic life.
[17] Elam, for example, points out that Parks "constructs complex interactions between race, sexuality, economics, and culture," but pays little attention to the relation between economics and the other three categories (117).
[18] Here as elsewhere I date the plays by their first public performance. The chronology of the plays as texts is somewhat more complicated. Parks has described *In The Blood* as the "alien baby" of *Fucking A,* much of it coming to her while she was in the process of completing an earlier, much longer draft of *Fucking A* (Garrett 134).
[19] This notion of embodying language is present in most of Parks's work. See for example Louis's discussion of *The Death of the Last Black Man in the Whole Entire World.*
[20] Critics seem to disagree as to which of the two plays is more Brechtian. Geis, for instance, calls *In the Blood* "a somewhat more naturalistic play" than *Fucking A* (127). Schafer describes *Fucking A* as "Brechtian epic theatre" and describes *In the Blood* as "classical tragedy in a contemporary setting" (182). Foster sees *Fucking A's* plot as more "classically Aristotelian" (82). In fact, both plays rely heavily on the Brechtian techniques I've listed.
[21] Patterson's piece cites recent contributions to this critique of authenticity by James Nolan, Richard Sennett, and Philip Rieff.

Bibliography

The Apprentice. NBC. 2004 - Present.

Aristotle. *Politics.* Trans. Benjamin Jowett. New York: The Modern Library, 1943.

Austin, John L. *How to Do Things with Words.* 2nd ed. Cambridge: Harvard U.P., 1975.

Barish, Jonas. *The Antitheatrical Prejudice.* Berkeley: U. of California Press, 1981.

Barthes, Roland. *S/Z.* Trans. Richard Miller. New York: Hill and Wang, 1974.

Benn Michaels, Walter. *The Gold Standard and the Logic of Naturalism: American Literature at the Turn of the Century.* Berkeley: University of California Press, 1987.

Berkman, Len. "Language as Protagonist in *In the Blood.*" Wetmore 61-72.

Bigsby, C.W.E. *David Mamet. Contemporary Writers* series. Ed. Malcolm Bradbury and Christopher Bigsby. London and New York: Methuen, 1985.

Bogumil, Mary L. "'Tomorrow Never Comes': Songs of Cultural Identity in August Wilson's 'Joe Turner's Come and Gone'." Theatre Journal 46:4 (Dec. 1994) 463-476.

—. *Modern American Drama: 1945 – 2000.* 2nd ed. Cambridge, UK: Cambridge University Press, 2000.

Bloom, Harold. *Willy Loman. Major Literary Characters* Series. New York: Chelsea House, 1991.

Brantley, Ben. "A Woman Named Hester, Wearing a Familiar Letter." *The New York Times* 17 March 2003. Nytimes.com. Web. 23 Oct. 2009.

Callens, Johan. "Mr. Smith Goes to Chicago: Playing Out Mamet's Critique of Capitalism in *American Buffalo.*" *European Journal of American Culture* 19.1(2000): 17-29.

Canby, Vincent. "A Side-by-Side Contrast of Solemn and Lively." *The New York Times* 19 Dec. 1999: AR7. Proquest. Web. 23 Oct. 2009.

Cannan, E. et al. "Who Said 'Barren Metal'? A Symposium." *Economica* 5 (June 1922) 105-111.

Carnegie, Dale. *How To Win Friends And Influence People.* New York: Pocket Books, 1982.

Casty, Alan Howard. *The Gangster and the American Social Drama of the Thirties: a Study of the Interaction of an Icon of Popular Culture and the Conventions of Drama.* Unpublished Dissertation. University of California, Los Angeles, 1973.

Chaudhuri, Una. Rev. of *Topdog/Underdog*, by Suzan-Lori Parks. *Theatre Journal* 54.2 (2002) 289-291.

Dean, Anne. *David Mamet: Language as Dramatic Action.* Rutherford: Fairleigh Dickinson UP, 1990.

"*Death of a Salesman:* A Symposium." Bloom 43-49.

Delbaere-Garant, Jeanne. "Psychic Realism, Mythic Realism, Grotesque Realism: Variations on Magical Realism in Contemporary Literature in English." Zamora, Lois Parkinson and Faris, Wendy B., eds. *Magical Realism: Theory, History, Community.* Durham, NC: Duke UP, 1005. 249-63.

Demastes, William. *Beyond Naturalism: A New Realism in American Theatre.* Troy, MO: Greenwood, 1988.

Dietrick, Jon. "Real Classical Money: Naturalism and David Mamet's *American Buffalo. Twentieth-Century Literature*. 52.3 (Fall 2006).

Eisinger, Chester E. "Focus on *Death of a Salesman." American Dreams, American Nightmares.* Ed. David Madden. Carbondale: Southern Illinois University Press, 1970. 165-74.

Elam, Harry J. "The Postmulticultural: A Tale of Mothers and Sons." Maufort, Marc. *Crucible of Cultures: Anglophone Drama at the Dawn of a New Millenium.* Brussel, Belgium: Peter Lang, 2002. 113-28.

—. "Theatre of the Gut: Tennessee Williams and Susan-Lori Parks." *The Influence of Tennessee Williams: Essays on Fifteen American Playwrights.* Ed. Philip C. Kolin. Jefferson: McFarland, 2008. 200-15.

Executive Suite. Dir. Robert Wise. Perf. William Holden, June Allyson, Barbara Stanwyck, Frederic March. 1954. Videocassette. MGM Video, 1998.

"Explosive Play Hits the Sleepy Theatre." Rev. of *Dead End,* by Sidney Kingsley. *Literary Digest.* 9 Nov. 1935: 17.

Frank, Haike. "The Instability of Meaning in Suzan-Lori Parks' *The America Play. American Drama* 11.2 (2002): 4-20.

Fearnow, Mark. *The American Stage and the Great Depression: A Cultural History of the Grotesque. Cambridge Studies in American Theatre and Drama.* Series Ed. Don B. Wilmeth. Cambridge: Cambridge University Press, 1997.

Foster, Verna A. "Nurturing and Murderous Mothers in Suzan-Lori Parks's *In the Blood* and *Fucking A*. *American Drama* 16:1. 75-89.
Freud, Sigmund. *Beyond the Pleasure Principle*. Trans. James Strachey. New York: Norton, 1961.
—. "The 'Uncanny.'" *General Psychological Theory: Papers on Metapsychology*. Ed. Philip Rieff. New York: Macmillan, 1963. 122-161.
Fuchs, Elinor. "Presence and the Revenge of Writing: Rethinking Theatre after Derrida." *Performing Arts Journal* 9:2 (1995): 163-173.
Gardner, R.H. "Tragedy of the Lowest Man." *The Splintered Stage*. New York: MacMillan, 1965. 122-134.
Garrett, Shawn-Marie. "The Possession of Suzan-Lori Parks." *American Theatre* 17:8 (Oct. 2000): 22-26, 132-34.
Geis, Deborah R. *Suzan-Lori Parks*. Ann Arbor: U. of Michigan Press, 2008.
Gene Simmons Family Jewels. A&E. 2006.
Germana, Michael. *Standards of Value: Money, Race, and Literature in America*. Iowa City, IA: U. of Iowa Press, 2009.
Goldstein, Malcolm. *Political Stage: American Drama and Theater of the Great Depression*. New York: Oxford University Press, 1974.
Goux, Jean-Joseph. "Cash, Check, or Charge?" *The New Economic Criticism*. Ed. Martha Woodmansee and Mark Osteen. Economics as Social Theory. Ser. Ed. Tony Lawson. London: Routledge, 1999. 114-127.
—. *Symbolic Economies: After Marx and Freud*. Trans. Jennifer Curtiss Gage. Ithaca, NY: Cornell University Press, 1990.
Greenspan, Alan. "Gold and Economic Freedom." *Capitalism: The Unknown Ideal*. By Ayn Rand. New York: New American Library, 1966. 89-95.
Hawthorne, Nathaniel. *The Scarlet Letter*. 3rd ed. New York: Norton, 1988.
Heidegger, Martin. "The Question Concerning Technology." Trans. William Lovitt. *Basic Writings*. Ed. David Farrell Krell. San Francisco: HarperCollins, 1993. 311-341.
Heinzelman, Kurt. *The Economics of the Imagination*. Amherst: The University of Massachusetts Press, 1980.
Hoeller, Hildegard. "Racial Currency: Zora Neale Hurston's 'The Gilded Six-Bits' and the Gold-Standard Debate." *American Literature: A Journal of Literary History, Criticism, and Bibliography* 2005 Dec; 77 (4): 761-85.

Hofstadter, Richard. *Anti-intellectualism in American Life.* New York: Knopf, 1963.

Hornby, Richard. *Drama, Metadrama and Perception.* Lewisburg, PA: Bucknell University Press, 1986.

Isherwood, Charles. Rev. of *Fucking A*, dir. by Mark Greif. *Variety* 17 Mar. 2003: 6

Johung, Jennifer. "Figuring the 'Spells'/Spelling the Figures: Suzan-Lori Parks' 'Scene of Love (?).'" *Theatre Journal* 58.1 (2006) 39-52.

Kane, Leslie. *David Mamet in Conversation.* Ann Arbor: Univ. of Michigan Press, 2001.

Keynes, John Maynard. *The Collected Writings of John Maynard Keynes.* Vol. 4. *A Tract on Monetary Reform.* Cambridge: MacMillan, 1971.

Kimmel, Michael. *Manhood in America: A Cultural History.* New York: The Free Press, 1997.

King, Thomas L. "Talk and Dramatic Action in American Buffalo." *Modern Drama* 34.4 (1991): 538-48.

Kingsley, Sidney. *Dead End. Five Prizewinning Plays.* Ed. Nena Couch. *Theatre Studies.* Series Ed. Alan Woods and Nena Couch. Columbus: Ohio State University Press, 1995.77-166.

Kolin, Philip. *"Parks's In The Blood." The Explicator 64:4 (Summer 2006) 253-55.*

Krutch, Joseph Wood. "Sure Fire." Rev. of *Dead End,* by Sidney Kingsley. *The Nation.* 13 Nov. 1935: 57-58.

Louis, Yvette. "Body Language: The Black Female Body and the Word in Suzan-Lori Parks' *The Death of the Last Black Man in the Whole Entire World."* Bennett, Michael and Vanessa D. Dickerson. *Recovering the Black Female Body: Self-Representations by African American Women.* New Brunswick: Rutgers UP, 2001.

Mamet, David. *American Buffalo.* New York: Grove Press, 1996.

—. *The Cryptogram.* New York: Dramatists Play Service, 1995.

—. *Glengarry Glen Ross.* New York: Grove Press, 1984.

—. *House of Games: the Complete Screenplay.* New York: Grove Press, 1987.

—. *Some Freaks.* New York: Viking, 1989.

—. *South of the Northeast Kingdom.* Washington, DC: National Geographic Society, 2002.

—. dir. *The Spanish Prisoner.* Perf. Campbell Scott, Steve Martin, Rebecca Pidgeon, and Ben Gazzara. Sony, 1997.

—. *The Spanish Prisoner and The Winslow Boy: Two Screenplays.* New York: Vintage, 1998.

The Man in the Grey Flannel Suit. Dir. Nunnally Johnson. Perf. Gregory Peck, Jennifer Jones, Frederic March, Marisa Pavan, and Lee J. Cobb. 1956. DVD. Twentieth-Century FOX, 2005.

Marx, Karl. *Capital: A Critique of Political Economy.* Edited by Frederick Engels. Trans. By Samuel Moore and Edward Aveling from 3rd German ed. 3 vols. New York: International Publishers, 1967.

—. *Economic and Philosophic Manuscripts of 1844.* Ed. Dirk J. Struik. Trans. Martin Milligan. New York: International Publishers, 1964.

—. *Writings of the Young Marx on Philosophy and Society.* Ed. And trans. By Loyd D. Easton and Kurt H. Guddat. Garden City, NY: Doubleday, 1967.

Maufort, Marc. "'A Rustle of Wind Blowing Across Two Continents': August Wilson's Magic Realism as Expression of Empowerment." *Voices of Power: Co-operation and Conflict in English Language and Literature.* Ed. Marc Maufort. Liege: English Dept. U of Liege, 1997. 173-181.

Miller, Arthur. *Death of a Salesman.* New York: Penguin, 1977.

—. *Timebends: A Life.* New York: Grove, 1987.

Miller, Jordan Y. "Myth and the American Dream: O'Neill to Albee." *Modern Drama,* 7 (September), 1964. 190-198.

Mills, C. Wright. *White Collar: The American Middle Classes.* New York: Oxford University Press, 1951.

Moss, Leonard. "Arthur Miller and the Common Man's Language." *Modern Drama.* 7(1). Summer 1964. 55-70.

Murphy, Brenda. *American Realism and American Drama, 1880—1940. Cambridge Studies in American Literature and Culture.* Series Ed. Albert Gelpi. Cambridge: Cambridge University Press, 1987.

—. "Willy Loman: Icon of Business Culture." *Michigan Quarterly Review.* 37(4). Fall 1998. 755-766.

Murphy, Brenda & Abbotson, Susan W. *Understanding* Death of a Salesman*: A Student Casebook to Issues, Sources, and Historical Documents. The Greenwood Press "Literature in Context" Series.* Ed. Claudia Durst Johnson. Westport, CT: Greenwood Press, 1999.

Norris, Frank. *McTeague: A Story of San Francisco.* New York: Penguin, 2003.

Oakes, Guy. *The Soul of the Salesman: The Moral Ethos of Personal Sales.* New Jersey: Humanities Press International, 1990.

O'Malley, Michael. *Face Value: The Entwined Histories of Money and Race in America.* Chicago: Univ. of Chicago Press, 2012.

—. Introduction to "Specie and Species: Race and the Money Question in Nineteenth-Century America." *American Historical Review*. April 1994. 369-395.

The Osbournes. MTV. 2002-2005.

Oxford English Dictionary Online. 2nd ed. 1989. University of CT Lib., Storrs, CT. <http://dictionary.oed.com>.

Parks, Suzan-Lori. "From *Elements of Style*." *The America Play and Other Works*. New York: Theatre Communications Group, 1995. 6-18.

Parks, Suzan-Lori. *Fucking A. The Red Letter Plays*. New York: Theatre Communications Group, 2001. 113-242.

—. *In The Blood. The Red Letter Plays*. New York: Theatre Communications Group, 2001. ix-112.

—. *Topdog/Underdog*. New York: Dramatists Play Service, 2002.

Patterson, Orlando. "Our Overrated Inner Self." *The New York Times* Tuesday 16 Dec. 2006: A35.

Piette, Alain. "The Flexing of Muscles and Tongues: Thug Rituals and Rhetoric in David Mamet's *American Buffalo." Crucible of Cultures: Anglophone Drama at the Dawn of a New Millennium*. Ed. Marc Manfort and Franca Bellarsi. Brussels: P.I.E.-Peter Lund, SA, 2002. 91-100.

Poggi, Gianfranco. *Money and the Modern Mind: Georg Simmel's* Philosophy of Money. Berkeley: University of California Press, 1993.

Rabkin, Gerald. *Drama and Commitment: Politics in the American Theatre of the Thirties. Indiana University Humanities Series No. 54*. Series Ed. Edward D. Seeber. Bloomington: Indiana University Press, 1964.

The Real Housewives of Orange County. BRAVO. 2006.

The Real World. MTV. 1992-Present.

Reynolds, R.C. *Stage Left: The Development of the American Social Drama in the Thirties*. Troy, NY: Whitson, 1986.

Rutherford, Jonathan. "Who's That Man?" *Male Order: Unwrapping Masculinity*. Ed. Chapman, Rowena and Jonathan Rutherford. London: Lawrence & Wishart, 1996. 21- 67.

Ryan, Katy. "'No Less Human': Making History in Suzan-Lori Parks'ss *The America Play*." *Journal of Dramatic Theory and Criticism* 13.2 (1999): 81-84.

Schafer, Carol. "Staging a New Literary History": *Comparative Drama* 42:2 (Summer 2008) 181-203.

Shakespeare, William. *The Merchant of Venice. The Complete Works of Shakespeare*. 4th ed. Ed. Bevington, David. New York: HarperCollins, 1992. 178-215.

Sheehan, Paul. "Marx, Money, and Monstrosity in *Great Expectations.*" *Q/W/E/R/T/Y: Arts, Litteratures & Civilisations du Monde Anglophone* 9:1999. 97-104.

Shell, Marc. *The Economy of Literature.* Baltimore: Johns Hopkins U.P., 1978.

—. *Money, Language, and Thought: Literary and Philosophical Economies from the Medieval to the Modern Era.* Baltimore: Johns Hopkins U.P., 1993.

Shorris, Earl. *A Nation of Salesmen: The Tyranny of the Market and the Subversion of Culture.* New York: Norton, 1994.

Simmel, Georg. *The Philosophy of Money.* Ed. David Frisby. Trans. Tom Bottomore and David Frisby. London: Routledge, 1990.

Simon, John. "Expletive Committed." *New York* 36:11 (March 2003): 56.

Siracusa, Joseph M. and Coleman, David G. *Depression to Cold War: A History of America from Herbert Hoover to Ronald Reagan. Perspectives on the Twentieth Century* series. Series Advisor, Edward Beauchamp. Westport, Connecticut: Praeger, 2002.

Solomon, William. *Literature, Amusement and Technology in the Great Depression. Cambridge Studies in American Literature and Culture.* Series Ed. Ross Posnock. New York: Cambridge University Press, 2002.

The Spanish Prisoner. Dir. David Mamet. Perf. Campbell Scott, Steve Martin, Rebecca Pidgeon, and Ben Gazzara. Sony Pictures, 1997.

Spears, Timothy. *100 Years on the Road: The Traveling Salesman in American Culture.* New Haven: Yale University Press, 1995.

The Surreal Life. VH1. 2003-Present.

Thompson, E.P. "Time, Work-Discipline, and Industrial Capitalism." *Past and Present* 38 Dec. 1967, 56-97.

Wanniski, Jude. *The Way the World Works.* Wash., DC: Regnery, 1998.

Weber, Max. *The Protestant Ethic and the "Spirit" of Capitalism.* Ed. and Trans. Peter Baehr and Gordon C. Wells. New York: Penguin, 2002.

Wetmore, Kevin J., Jr. and Alycia Smith-Howard. *Suzan-Lori Parks: A Casebook.* New York: Routledge, 2007.

Williams, Keith and Matthews, Steven, eds. *Rewriting the Thirties: Modernism and After. Studies in Twentieth-Century Literature.* Series ed. Stan Smith. London and New York: Longman, 1997.

Williams, Kirk. "Anti-Theatricality and the Limits of Naturalism." *Against Theatre: Creative Destructions on the Modern Stage.* Ed. Alan Ackerman and Martin Puchner. New York: Palgrave MacMillan, 2006. 95-111.

Williams, Raymond. "Modern Tragic Literature: From Hero to Victim." Bloom 15.

—. *The Country and the City.* New York: Oxford University Press, 1973.

Wilson, August. *Joe Turner's Come and Gone.* New York: Penguin, 1988.

Wilson, Robert. "The Salesman and Society." From *The Writer as Social Seer.* Chapel Hill: University of North Carolina Press, 1979. 57-71.

Worster, David. "How to Do Things with Salesmen: David Mamet's Speech-Act Play." *David Mamet's* Glengarry Glen Ross*: Text and Performance.* Ed. Leslie Kane. New York: Garland, 1996. 63-79.

Worthen, W.B. "Citing History: Textuality and Performativity in the Plays of Suzan-Lori Parks." *Essays in Theatre/Etudes Theatrales* 18.1 (1999): 3-22.

Young, Harvey. "Choral Compassion: *In the Blood* and *Venus.* Wetmore 29-47.

INDEX

A

antitheatrical prejudice, 8–9
Aristotle, 5, 6, 90, 111, 117, *See* Money: monstrosity
Artaud, Antonin, 64
authenticity, 127–33

B

Barish, Jonas, 9
Barthes, Roland, 38
Bel Geddes, Norman, 24
Benn Michaels, Walter, 1, 2, 5, 6, 8, 10, 53, 98, 106, 109, *See* logic of naturalism
Bigsby, Christopher, 33, 52
blood money, 19–20, 26
Bloom, Harold, 44
Bowery Boys, The, 138
Brantley, Ben, 108
Brecht, Berthold, 108, 110, 124

C

Cagney, James, 138
Canby, Vincent, 107
Carnegie, Dale, 46
Casty, Alan, 9
Cather, Willa, 29, 67
Chappelle, Dave, 96–98
Coleman, David G., 138
Crane, Stephen, 67, 80

D

Dean, Anne, 138
Delbaere, Jeanne, 80–81
Demastes, William, 12, 13
Diverse Works/Infernal Bridegroom Productions, 108
Dreiser, Theodore, 12, 67, 70, 80
Dubois, W.E.B., 98
Dworkin, Martin, 47

E

Eisinger, Chester E., 138
Esbjornson, David, 107
expressionism, 12, 67

F

Federal Theatre Project, 15
Foster, Hal, 21
Freud, 138
Freud, Sigmund, 2, 27, 59
Fuchs, Elinor, 8

G

Gardner, R.H., 33
Gene Simmons Family Jewels, 128
Germana, Michael, 79, 96
gold standard, 1, 7–8, 10, 36, 53, 76, 78–79, 114, 117–18, 125
Goldstein, Malcolm, 15
Goux, Jean-Joseph, 2, 7, 78, 88, 89, 109, 114, 118
Greenspan, Alan, 138
Greif, Michael, 108

H

Haike, Frank, 105
Hawthorne, Nathaniel, 80, 108, 113
Heidegger, Martin, 44–45, 47, 74
Heinzelman, Kurt, 62

Hellman, Lillian, 138
Hoeller, Hildegaard, 10, 138
Hofstadter, Richard, 30
Hogan Knows Best, 128
Hornby, Richard, 24

I

Isherwood, Charles, 108

K

Kane, Leslie, 63, 64
Kazan, Elia, 12
Keynes, John Maynard, 7
King, Thomas L., 51, 62, 138
Kingsley, Sidney, 9, 11, 15–27, 57, 125–26, 129
Kolin, Philip, 112
Krasner, David, 107
Krutch, Joseph Wood, 24

L

Lacan, Jacques, 2
language and action, 33–34, 51, 54, 56–57, 60–63, 76–79, 86–88, 114–17
logic of naturalism, 8, 11, 13, 27, 29, 36, 50, 53, 57, 63, 64, 71, 81, 82, 86, 93, 98, 103, 106, 109, 126, 127

M

magical realism, 69, 80–81
Mamet, David, 106
- *American Buffalo,* 10, 11, 12, 49–67, 76, 91, 125, 126
- *Five Cities of Refuge,* 66
- *Glengarry Glen Ross,* 48, 64
- *House of Games,* 54
- *Some Freaks,* 64
- *South of the Northeast Kingdom,* 65
- *The Cryptogram,* 54
- *The Spanish Prisoner,* 55

Marx, Karl, 3–4, 57, 62
Maufort, Marc, 80–81
metadrama, 12, 24, 102
Miller, Arthur
- *Death of a Salesman,* 10, 11, 12, 56, 57, 87, 126–27
- *Timebends,* 10, 30, 36

Miller, Jordan, 33
Mills, C. Wright, 32, 46
minstrelsy, 95–98
money
- and art, 59
- and honor, 25–26
- and identity, 18–27, 76–79, 83, 92–95, 113–14, 120
- and monstrosity, 19, 22, 61–62, 90, 110, 111
- and neutrality, 2, 26, 57–58
- and race, 78–79, 85–124
- and sexuality, 62, 88–91, 121–22

Murphy, Brenda, 12, 26, 43

N

naturalism, 12–13, 80–81, *See* logic of naturalism
New Deal, 15
new realism, 12–13
Norris, Frank, 8, 12, 53, 70, 103

O

O'Malley, Michael, 6
O'Malley, Michael, 6, 7, 78, 79
Oakes, Guy, 34, 35, 47, 48
Odets, Clifford, 108
Osbournes, The, 128

P

paper money, 6, 36
Papp, Joseph Public Theater, 107, 108

Parks, Suzan-Lori
"Elements of Style", 12, 85, 105, 106
Fucking A, 117–24
In the Blood, 107–17
The America Play, 93
Topdog/Underdog, 11, 12, 85, 127, 130
Patterson, Orlando, 129
Piette, Alain, 138
Poggi, Gianfranco, 3, 7, 38, 96
Popular Front, 15

R

Rabkin, Gerald, 15
Real Housewives of Orange County, The, 128
Real World, The, 128
realism, 12–13, 24, 63, 80–81, 107, 124
Reynolds, R.C., 15
Rice, Elmer, 15, 67
Richards, Lloyd, 69
Ryan, Katy, 105

S

Shaw, Irwin, 15
Shell, Marc, 1–2, 5, 20, 23, 109, 118
Sherwood, Robert E., 15
Shorris, Earl, 30, 42
Simmel, Georg, 2–3, 5, 7, 18, 20, 23, 26, 27, 37, 38, 39, 40, 47, 49, 58, 61, 96, 138
Simon, John, 108
Siracusa, Joseph, 138
Smith, Adam, 117
Solomon, William, 21
Spears, Timothy, 29–30, 29, 42–43
speech and action, 31–32
Stanislavski, Konstantin, 63
supply-side economics, 7, 8
Surreal Life, The, 128
Survivor, 128

T

Theatre Union, 9, 15
theft, 40
Thompson, E.P., 41, 42, 45

U

uncanny, 19, 35, 40, 47–48, 57, 83, 92, 94, 101, 126, 128, *See* Heidegger, Martin

V

violence and economic life, 34–35

W

Weber, Max, 42
Williams, Raymond, 38, 42
Wilson, August, 10, 12, 69–83, 127
Worster, David, 138
Worthen, W.B., 106

Y

Yale Repertory Theatre, 69
Young, Harvey, 124